TRENCH FEVER

TRENCH
FEVER

CHRISTOPHER
MOORE

LITTLE, BROWN AND COMPANY

A *Little, Brown* Book

First published in Great Britain by
Little, Brown and Company 1998

Copyright © Christopher Moore 1998

The moral right of the author has been asserted.

A CIP catalogue record for this book
is available from the British Library.

ISBN 0 316 64696 2

Map copyright © Neil Hyslop

Typeset in Bembo by
Palimpsest Book Production Limited,
Polmont, Stirlingshire
Printed and bound in Great Britain by
Clays Ltd, St Ives plc

Little, Brown and Company (UK)
Brettenham House
Lancaster Place
London WC2E 7EN

To Catriona, always

CONTENTS

ACKNOWLEDGEMENTS

I gratefully acknowledge permission to quote from the following works: 'Long Goodbye for the Legions Lost' by Stephen Bates, by permission of the *Guardian* newspaper; 'Under Fire' by Henri Barbusse, by permission of Everyman's Library, publishers; 'Undertones of War' by Edmund Blunden, reprinted by permission of The Peters Fraser and Dunlop Group Ltd; 'To the Unknown Warrior' by G.K. Chesterton, reprinted by permission of A.P. Watt Ltd. on behalf of the Royal Literary Fund; 'A True and Unexaggerated Report' by Captain Robert Fieldsend, from *Gun Fire No. 17*, edited by A.J. Peacock, by permission of A.J. Peacock; 'Mesopotamia' by Rudyard Kipling, by permission of A.P. Watt Ltd. on behalf of The National Trust; 'Disenchantment' by C.E. Montague, by permission of Harper Collins Publishers; 'Spring Offensive' and 'Miners' by Wilfred Owen, from *Poems of Wilfred Owen*, edited by Jon Stallworthy, by permission of Random House, publishers; 'Margin Released' by J.B. Priestley by permission of The Peters Fraser and Dunlop Group Ltd; 'Of Those We Loved' by I.L. Read, by permission of Captain R.C. Read, CBE, FRICS, Royal Navy (Retd); 'The Kiss' and 'To Any Dead Soldier' by Siegfried Sassoon; copyright © Siegfried

Sassoon, by permission of George Sassoon; 'The Great War' by Vernon Scannell, from *New and Collected Poems 1952–1980*, by permission of Robson Books, publishers; 'I had a Rendezvous with Death' by Alan Seeger, from *Poems by Alan Seeger*, copyright © 1916 by Charles Scribner's Sons, renewed 1944 by Elsie Adams Seeger and 'Going Home' by Robert Service, courtesy of the Estate of Robert Service.

The author also gratefully acknowledges permission to reprint Crown Copyright material in respect of records held in the Public Record Office, Kew, and excerpts from the *Official History of The Great War* (Military Operations, France and Belgium 1916, Volume One, by Brigadier-General Sir James E. Edmunds, C.B, C.M.G, R.E. (Retd), p.s.c.). Crown copyright material is reproduced with the permission of the Controller of Her Majesty's Stationery Office. I am happy to acknowledge my debt to the following two works, the copyright holders of which I have been unable to trace: *Footprints of the 1/4th Leicestershire Regiment*, by Captain John Milne, and *The Fifth Leicestershire*, by Captain J.D. Hills. Without these two battalion histories it would not have been possible to piece together Walter Butterworth's likely movements on the Western Front.

My personal thanks go to: Bill Jackson and Piers Pool, good friends on the battlefield; Peter Butterworth and the late Clive Butterworth (Uncle Mick), who provided valuable recollections of Walter; and Shirley Butterworth and Carolyn Moore, who supplied guidance and useful research. Most of all I want to thank my wife and children for three years' support, encouragement and chocolate. I apologise for any mistakes, omissions or inaccuracies in *Trench Fever*, the responsibility for which is entirely my own.

CGM

TRENCH
FEVER

1

THE TICKET

Whenever war is spoken of
I find
The war that was called Great invades the mind . . .
Vernon Scannell, 'The Great War'

The battle is over, the War continues. On quiet nights, if the wind is from the east, you can still hear that sinister barrage. In the churchyard of Christ the King on Shooters Hill, London SE18, stands the proud milestone: '8 miles to London Bridge, 7 miles to Dartford, 130 miles to Ypres. In defending The Salient our casualties were 90,000 killed, 70,500 missing, 410,000 wounded.'

One week after landing, Walter Butterworth was at Plugstreet, eight miles south of Ypres town. His regiment was attached to a battalion of Lancashire Fusiliers to learn the rudiments of trench fighting. The first casualty was Second-Lieutenant Aked, a platoon commander in 'C' Company, drilled through the head by a sniper. He died where he dropped two hours after entering his first trench. Walter was in a front-line fire bay when the news came along. One of the men in his section wondered aloud if they shouldn't do something.

'Do?'

Walter's novices looked away from the sarcastic lance-corporal and fiddled with bits of equipment.

'Name like that?' sneered the lance-jack. 'He had it coming—' He held his finger to his head and cocked his thumb. '—Mister Ache 'ead.'

The Lancashires sniggered, Walter's men felt confused. They'd been told to be proud that they were the first Territorials to go overseas as a complete division. Walter gulped his tea and found it surprisingly hot and sweet.

'That's good,' he said.

A runner hustled past to rouse the sergeants. The Lancashires spat their wads and handled their weapons expertly in the gathering gloom; Walter's men fumbled and cursed. At the order 'Stand To Arms', the trench filled with grumblers. A field-gun coughed somewhere behind the German lines and there was a simultaneous explosion about 100 yards to the right of where Walter had his eye pressed to a notch in the sandbags. Two Lancashires scampered back from their observation post with their arses in the air, to hoots of derision from their comrades. The British artillery, wherever it was, remained quiet.

On receiving the order 'Fire At Will', Walter released the safety-catch on his rifle and peered through his loophole for a target. Ripe, sooty fumes drifted slowly downwind from the crater where the German shell had exploded. Shadows flitted across the bumps and hollows of No Man's Land. Fire at will at what? The battlefield was empty. Walter steadied the stock of his rifle against his cheek and took aim at a clump of weeds. Sixty-three close-fitting parts awaited his command, tip of the foresight in line with the backsight. The remembered voice of Sergeant Templeman echoed in his inner ear: 'Squeeze it, lad, don't jerk it. It's not a wanking competition.'

Walter took aim at what he hoped was a piece of the German parapet and fired. It was just like training. His head cleared wonderfully. Then a German ricochet whirred past and he ducked.

'Dinna shit tha'sen,' scolded the Lancashire next to him.

A German machine gun opened up and everybody crouched as low as Walter. Bullets thudded into the topmost sandbags of the breastwork at 2,000 miles per hour and spent themselves in the muddy sump of the trench bottom. The spent bullets were heavy and wrinkled, like fat grey raisins. Walter picked one up when he thought no one was looking. The strafe continued – efficient traverses from the German machine-gunners, hectic potting from the British fusiliers – until a flurry of rapid fire announced that the snipers on both sides had emptied their magazines to formally end another cramp-inducing shift. The British 'Stood Down' and posted sentries.

Walter lay on compacted mud that night, unable to sleep. His comrades' elbows and knees jabbed back every time he wriggled for a more comfortable position. He had realised that, contrary to his previous inner conviction, he was going to get hit. They were all going to get hit. Walter felt for the superstitious nugget in his breast pocket, the machine-gun bullet that hadn't had his name on it. He mourned for the life he'd given to the War, that anonymous life which was now so expendable. He thought of Lieutenant Aked and the clumsy lack of ceremony with which his boyish corpse had been despatched to the burial plot, straight from his posh school to a watery grave, with barely a mark on his beautiful uniform.

Already, Plugstreet Wood was dotted with impromptu British cemeteries.

The date was March 6th 1915, and Walter was two weeks away from his 24th birthday. At home, in Hinckley, Leicestershire, he'd left a wife, Clara, and a son he'd never seen, Walter Noël Gordon, born on Christmas Day 1914.

Great War fact or Great War fiction? Walter is a fact, my grandfather. Plugstreet is a fact, where Walter slept on compacted mud on the night of March 6th 1915. The presence of the Lancashire Fusiliers is indisputably historical, as is the manner of death of Second-Lieutenant Aked. All these facts are verifiable from written sources. The sarcastic lance-corporal is not. I made him up, or borrowed him from someone else's book. I have had a surfeit of public school types dying tragically on the wire. I can no longer suspend my disbelief. Sassoon, Graves and Blunden said it for the subalterns; Manning, Coppard and Richards said it for the other ranks. Fiction doesn't do it for me any more. I have yet to find the Great War book which explains why it matters so much, why I still catch myself, when the wind is from the east, listening for the barrage at Ypres?

It began in a classroom high on a hill with a distant view of a power-station smokestack. We were reading the War Poets for O-level. For the first time in my inky, football-crazed life I was about to be knocked sideways by a work of art: 'Dulce Et Decorum Est' by Wilfred Owen. As we read the words aloud, my boy's store of feelings overflowed without warning. It had to be stopped. I choked on the injustice. That night I read all the War Poets in the textbook and learned 'Dulce Et Decorum Est' by heart.

I identified with Owen's gassed Englishmen to the extent of an overwhelming pity, but I was also jealous that I had been denied a chance to suffer with them. I was old enough for irony, but the physical impact of Owen's words went deeper. His gassed men had died for me in a straight swap, their future for mine. Death by German phosgene did not diminish them. If England was worth fighting for, then '*Dulce Et Decorum Est Pro Patria Mori*' could not be a lie.

That was the year, whenever it was, that books came alive for me. I plundered Dunfermline's public library for books about the Great War, traversed it from the Eastern Front to Caporetto, the Balkans to East Africa. Yet these chapter headings, like those on 'The Genesis Of The Tank' or 'The War In The Air', left my emotions tepid. 'The Tragedy Of Gallipoli' offered an interesting change of scenery, but I was quick to realise that the real drama, the decisive theatre, was the Western Front. I pored over the photographs. It seemed barely conceivable that, within living memory, men had been allowed to do such things to each other. It was fascinating to learn what bombs and bullets could do to the human body. I peered into craters full of mangled limbs, gawped at tatters blown into high branches.

When the Great War books ran out I kept on going, rescuing myself from morbidity with *Catcher in the Rye*, *Down and Out in Paris and London* and *Lucky Jim*. Kerouac and Sartre offered glimpses of further possibilities. I quit the Boy Scouts. At university, wilting under peer pressure, I signed up to Pacifism. I neglected my studies and wormed my way on to the student newspaper. The symptoms of trench fever lay dormant until I arrived in London to start my first job.

I was supposed to be a feature writer on *Cosmopolitan* magazine, except no one could tell me what a feature was or how to write one. I used to take novels to work to read in the lavatory. The highlight of the working day was my lunch-hour ramble around streets named after Western Front trenches. Doorways and doorknobs invoked the final exits of unknown heroes. I trod their footsteps. Kerbstones and keystones spoke to me. I walked with my neck out, checking pediments and lintels for dates that would refer me back to 1914–1918. None of which was of the slightest use at *Cosmopolitan*, so I was invited to forge my destiny elsewhere.

By the time I got married the condition was permanent. Our first holiday as man and wife included a bicycle tour of the British war cemeteries of the Ypres Salient. It came as a surprise to my wife to realise she had married a nerd. She should have examined my bookshelves more closely. I had come to believe that the Great War defined something ineradicably English about me and the family into which I had been born. The psychological mutations wrought on the Western Front had entered the gene pool. My somewhat embattled way of looking at the world – the ready assumption of the defensive posture, the instinctive mistrust of strangers and 'authority' – was the inheritance of trench warfare. Life was short. If anything could go wrong, it would. Never trust an officer. Never volunteer. Never welsh. Get your retaliation in first. Keep your head down.

These days I earn my living as a news editor. I sit wondering what to say about Rwanda, or Sri Lanka, or the single European currency. Every five or ten minutes a squawk box in the ceiling announces the imminent arrival of some new eruption of doom or dullness for the hourly bulletins. It's not a bad job, if you like that sort of thing, which I do. The building where I work is surrounded by Great War mementoes, like the inscription on the wall of India House at knee height: '1917–1919. American Young Men's Christian Association. This tablet marks the site of Eagle Hut where services to men of the American and Allied forces testified to the friendship of the English-speaking peoples.'

Was the Eagle Hut one of those places where American and

Canadian troops first exchanged their convivial packets of cocaine and cannabis with their British comrades? While their officers thronged the panelled bar – the Gaiety Bar – of the Waldorf Hotel across the road? Before falling in, tipsily, for the march to Waterloo or Charing Cross stations? Before catching the trains that would take them to the ferries that would take them to the trains that would take them to the trenches? Sozzled or sober, did the English-speaking allies pause on leaving the Eagle Hut to snatch a glimpse of the chorus girls at the stage door of the Gaiety Theatre . . . ?

The Gaiety is a bank today, the severely functional British headquarters of a Wall Street outfit. At the back of the building, six storeys above the pavement, stands a chorus of allegorical figures. No one who wasn't looking for them would know they were there: a life-sized Minerva, sworded for the fight; a blindfold Justice, uplifting her scales; a plumptious Maternity, nurturing the next generation; and Peace, bearing the palm of prosperity. You have to peer hard to decipher this sisterhood's message: 'War To Uphold The Right Peace'.

From the Aldwych, I head for the River Thames, cutting down through the cobbled communication trench of Savoy Hill to the support line of Embankment Gardens, down past the hindmost parts of the Savoy Hotel, musing over the sad life and fast times of the actress Billie Carleton, the proto flapper-girl whose taste in diaphanous stage wear made her the favourite pin-up of many a front-line dugout. Billie lived out her final months in an apartment in Savoy Court. One night at the end of 1918, after returning in the early hours from a ball to celebrate the Armistice, she died in her sleep of a cocaine overdose, setting a showbiz trend that was never to go out of style.

The Great War memorial on the Embankment was a gift from the people of Belgium in gratitude for Britain taking in 400,000

Belgian refugees, and for the 1,000,000 British dead and 2,000,000 British wounded which it cost to recoup the Belgian homeland from German invasion. In appreciation of this expenditure, a stretch of London pavement was chosen to receive a bronze statue of a mother and her children bearing tributary garlands. Justice pointed at a scroll, no doubt emblematic of the Treaty of London, of 1839, under which France, Prussia and Britain swore to defend Belgian neutrality. On the other side knelt Honour, a knight in armour, St George of course, resting his right hand on a sheathed sword – ready to strike should Justice be betrayed. As it was.

This monument to British Justice and Honour attracts little attention from the German tourists for whom the Embankment is a focus of their London itinerary. This spot, near Cleopatra's Needle, is where the safari-liveried coaches (Schumacher Reizen, Schmidt Touristik) await their passengers' return from their Thames river cruises. I have occasionally seen furtive couples snogging in the shelter of the Belgian monument, but I cannot recall anyone looking at it for its own sake. The stone used in its construction was cheap; the passage of years has corroded the details and Honour's face is entirely eaten away.

There's always something worth watching on the Thames, even if it's only Westminster's garbage heading downstream on a raft of barges. During the tourist season, Cleopatra's Needle swarms with young Pomeranians and Prussians taking photographs of each other. A plaque beneath one of the obelisk's watchful sphinxes explains that the scars on the masonry were caused by a bomb dropped during the first German air-raid on London on September 4th 1917. Someone, I notice, has attempted to rewrite history by scratching out the word 'German' and covering it with chewing gum.

My wife tells me I shouldn't take it so personally. She is embarrassed that I bear a personal grudge against the Kaiser and all drivers of Volkswagens, Audis, Mercedes, BMWs and Porsches. The individual Germans I know, I like. Why mention the War? But this chewing-gum thing . . .

War is bad. Peace is good. But sometimes you have to fight. The Germans broke their promise and invaded Belgium in 1914 because it was the most expedient way of attacking France. The French were spoiling for a fight and the British resigned to joining them, as per treaty. But in 1914 it was the Germans who had planned most assiduously for war, who had remorselessly trained and equipped for it, who exulted the loudest in launching it. Germany fought the Great War to dominate; France fought for revenge; Britain fought for Belgium.

As an adult, I had to recognise that my Great War obsession put me in the same sad category as fans of the Eurovision Song Contest and collectors of beer-bottle labels. I learned to keep quiet at dinner parties. I suspected that I might be working towards a Great War book of my own, but had no idea what shape it might take. During a telephone conversation with my widowed mother in Leicester, initiated by me to thank her for a gift token that I had spent on another book about the Battle of the Somme, she reminded me that my grandad had been there. It was something I had always known, but had somehow forgotten.

'What did he say?'

'He never talked about it. I was too young. By the time the War ended I was the only one at home.'

My mother was talking about the War you grew up in if you were born in 1935 and named after Shirley Temple.

'What regiment was he in?'

'He was with the Leicesters, I think.'

'Which battalion?'

'Give over,' said my mother. 'How on earth should I know?'

A battalion was 1,000 men. At the beginning of the Great War most British infantry regiments consisted of two battalions, one of which would be serving at home, the other in the Empire. By the end of the War, some county regiments had raised a dozen battalions or more. To stand any chance of finding Walter, I had to know his battalion.

'I told you,' said my mother. 'He didn't talk about the War. "Get off," he said. "Girls don't want to know about that stuff."'

'Didn't he talk about his pals? Didn't he go to reunions?'

The 1,000 men in an infantry battalion were divided into four companies under a Captain. Each company was divided into four platoons under a Lieutenant or Second-Lieutenant, the subaltern. Each platoon was divided into sections under a Sergeant or a Corporal. To find Walter, I needed to know which company he had been in, preferably which platoon. I needed his rank and regimental number. Had he been wounded? Had he won any medals?

'Ask your Uncle Peter,' said my mother. 'Ask Uncle Mick. He talked to the boys about it. All I know is, he was at the Somme.'

Of course he was. They were all at the Somme, England's finest.

'What sort of man was he?'

I felt ashamed of my ignorance. How could I have allowed myself to forget my own flesh and blood?

'He was a nice man.'

'Physically?'

'Walter? He was short and round. He was a little, round chap.'

He died when I was six months old. He had worked all his life in a shoe factory and had fathered six children, of whom the first-born – Walter Noël Gordon – died in adulthood of tuberculosis, while the last-born – my mother – was named after a Hollywood child star. All that my mother knew of Walter's military record was that he'd been at the Battle of the Somme with the Leicesters. On my next free weekend, I went back to visit Uncle Peter in Hinckley.

The hard facts consisted of two campaign medals, a miniature leather purse containing a 10-ore coin dated 1901, and a faded photograph of a soldier in uniform. These comprised the entirety of the Walter Butterworth Great War Archive. There were no letters, no diaries, no documents of any sort. When he died, Walter left nothing behind him in ink except the names of his children in the family Bible.

The photograph showed Walter as a short, stocky young man in the unadorned uniform of an infantry private – brass buttons, no badges, no chevrons. He had a challenging, sceptical look in his eye and a thick head of dark hair. Walter's forward-leaning stance, left arm akimbo, suggested suppressed energy and an inclination to cockiness. Walter's large-boned wife Clara, my grandmother-to-be, was seated alongside the young babe, Walter Noël Gordon. Gordon, as he was always to be known in the family, looked about 18 months old, which would date the photograph in the late summer or autumn of 1916. Walter's face and hands were suntanned, Clara's were not.

I weighed Walter's medals in the palm of my hand. The 1914–1915 Campaign medal was a dull bronze star with crossed swords. The 1914–1919 Victory medal felt as heavy as gold and was inscribed, 'The Great War for Civilization'. I was touching Walter for the first time since he'd held me as a baby. His name had been punched into the rim of each medal: L.Cpl Butterworth, W. B. 1650, Leics R.

'Do you know which battalion he was in?'

'The Fifth,' said Uncle Peter. 'Fifth Leicesters. The Fighting Fifth, that were your grandad's mob.'

'Do you know what company?'

Uncle Peter had been in the Army; he knew about divisions and brigades, battalions and companies.

'Nah,' he said. 'Nowt like that.'

Uncle Peter had stormed ashore with the Marines at Normandy in 1944. He knew a lot about war, but not much about Walter's.

'Did he mention any battles he was in?' I asked. 'He was at the Somme.'

'He were, yes. Mind you, they was all at the Somme. Biggest battle in history, the Somme. He were at all the big 'uns, your grandad.'

'Was he wounded?'

'Oh yes. He showed us the marks on his neck. Hill Sixty: Ypres. He were buried by a shell. They had to dig him out. The whole bloody lot of 'em was blown up and buried in the trench.'

Ypres. Uncle Peter pronounced it the way Walter must have done: 'Eep-rez'. Wipers, my arse. As far as the British Army was concerned, only those who had fought at Ypres in 1914 were qualified to called it Wipers. Uncle Peter had fought the Germans at Ypres in the Second World War.

'What about the purse?'

Walter must have picked it up on the battlefield, or looted it from a prisoner. Every man wore his lucky charm in battle, some amulet or token to ward off the evil chance. Was this Walter's? Where had he got it? What currency was the ore? What was the story?

'Took it off'n a dead Jerry, I expect,' said Uncle Peter. 'He killed a few on 'em, least he said he did. "It were me or the other bugger," that were your grandad's motto.'

★   ★   ★

I took Walter's details – Lance-Corporal, Fifth Leicesters, Regimental number 1650 – to the Public Record Office at Kew. If Uncle Peter was right and Walter had been wounded at Hill 60, there might be a record of it. I signed a form and was given an electronically impregnated swipe card permitting access to a great, air-conditioned reading room.

The Public Record Office retains a fraction of the tons of paperwork generated by the Royal Army Medical Corps on the Western Front between 1914 and 1918. Whenever a wounded soldier was transferred from one unit to another – from the makeshift Regimental Aid Post inside the fighting zone to one of the giant Base Hospitals on the French coast – his details were recorded in an Admissions Book, a small sample of which has been preserved. In addition, the Public Record Office holds a scattering of regimental medical records comprising the casualty slips and case histories of individual soldiers in individual battalions. Some 6 million men served in the British Army during the Great War. All of them received medical attention at some point. Yet partial records survive for only five regiments, and complete medical records for only two. The chance of finding the medical records of any randomly selected Great War soldier is therefore in the region of 10,000:1. It came as a shock to find Walter Butterworth after only twenty minutes.

It was an index card issued by Number 6 General Hospital, Expeditionary Force, France:

> Regiment: 5th. Leicester.
> Regimental Number: 1650.
> Troop, battery or company: D.
> Rank: Pte.
> Name: Butterworth W.B.
> Age: 25.

Service: 8.
Service (in Command or in Field Force): 14.
Disease: G.S.W. foot. Lt.
Admitted to Hospital: 19/4/16.
Discharged to Duty: 5/5/16.
Days under Treatment: 17.

It was like shaking hands with him, just the two of us, meeting quietly over the facts. The blood Walter had shed on the battlefield was in my veins.

'G.S.W. foot. Lt.' Did that mean a 'light' gunshot wound to the foot, or a gunshot wound to the 'left' foot? And why 'Pte'? Walter's medals gave his rank as Lance-Corporal.

Pinned to the medical records, with a rusty pin which had fused to the documents it held together, was the coarse Field Medical Card that Walter had carried from the battlefield. I smelled it reverently and held it up to the light. One of the Reading Room's security cameras twitched inquisitively in my direction. I had read in the newspaper of the sad collector of beer-bottle labels who'd been sentenced to a jail term for stealing specimens from Kew's collection.

'The reverse is to be used for notes on special cases (history, operations, special treatment or other necessary information); also on cases requiring or receiving special treatment during evacuation.'

The men used to call this card their ticket – to safety, to clean sheets, to Blighty, perhaps to Death.

'The red edged envelope will be used for cases dangerously or severely wounded and who require immediate attention.'

I turned the card over in my hands, seeking to absorb something from it, the *actualité*.

'If a more detailed history is necessary, a Medical Certificate (A.B. 172) or a Medical Case Sheet (A.F.I. 1237) or other statements of case may accompany.'

I examined Walter's ticket for bloodstains or tears. I put it back in the box and took it out again. I didn't want to see it returned to the vaults. I was the one who had searched for it; who had found it; who was uniquely placed to understand its significance. Walter's ticket away from the Western Front was my passport in the opposite direction.

I transcribed Walter's medical records into my notebook and sat dreaming for a few minutes. The presiding deity in my Great War pantheon, Siegfried Sassoon, had been usurped. Walter Butterworth was as different from Sig as it was possible for two Englishmen to be at the beginning of the twentieth century. Siegfried, with his exotic provenance and thoroughbred profile, epitomised the officer-poet. Walter was a wage slave in uniform. Siegfried, at the age of 25, commanded a private income of some £500 per annum. Walter was earning 25 shillings for a 60-hour week. It wasn't their blood that united them, but the fact that they were prepared to spill it for England.

'A label was attached to me,' says Siegfried of his Field Medical Card. 'I have kept that label and it is in my left hand as I write these words.'

'These words', because they were written in *Memoirs Of An Infantry Officer*, will live for ever. Walter's song stayed silent, except to his sons.

Somewhere in France or Flanders, Walter Butterworth had left his mark, and I was going to find it.

2

YPRES

For her was much accomplished, and she will not forget me,
Whose name is Legion . . .

                    Edmund Blunden, 'On Reading that the
               Rebuilding of Ypres Approached Completion'

After four days at Plugstreet, Walter and the Fifth Leicesters were marched south by a roundabout route to the village of Sailly-sur-la-Lys ('Sally-on-the-Loose') to be held in reserve for the Battle of Neuve Chapelle, the first full-dress British assault since the battles of movement of 1914 had given way to the siege conditions of the trenches. The French did not doubt the determination of the British to defend their lines, but did they have the stomach for a real fight?

The attack began at 0730 hours on March 10th 1915. A terse artillery bombardment – there weren't enough shells to stretch it to a whole hour – was followed by an infantry charge. With their Indian cohorts setting the pace, the British captured all their initial objectives, but faulty communications and indecision of command ensured that the breakthrough was not exploited. The acute shortage of artillery ammunition left the British infantry unprotected when the Germans regrouped for counter-attacks. Three days of fighting failed to secure an advance much beyond the gains of the first three hours. The final score was 13,000 casualties for the British, 14,000 for the Germans. In footballing terms — how else to visualise such crowds of young men? — Neuve Chapelle was a draw. The British had improved their standing with the French at the cost, in dead and wounded, of an average home gate for a down-table First Division side.

Not finding themselves called upon to fight at Neuve Chapelle, and no one having any more definite use for them, Walter and the Fifth Leicesters hung around the back lots of the First Army, digging trenches and getting wet until, on Easter Day 1915, they were ordered north to the Salient. Three weeks of marching in circles had brought them back within rifle range of where they'd started, and they still hadn't seen a German.

My prime source of facts about Walter's movements on the Western Front is the semi-official history of his battalion, *The Fifth Leicestershire. A record of the 1/5th Battalion the Leicestershire Regiment, T.F., during the War, 1914–1919.* The first chapter, covering the Fifth Leicesters' mobilisation and their six months of training in and around Luton, was written by Lieutenant-Colonel C.H. Jones, who commanded the battalion at the beginning of the War. After starting the book, and realising how much time it was going to take him to finish it, Jones handed the task to Captain J.D. Hills.

In peacetime, Colonel Jones had been a house-master at Leicestershire's nearest public school, Uppingham. This school on a hill, with its distant view of woods and pastures, is gilded by association with the doomed subalterns of Vera Brittain's classic, *Testament of Youth*. Colonel Jones invokes these associations explicitly in the way he introduces Captain Hills to his readers:

. . . John David Hills, though not twenty [when War was declared], had already seen six years' service in his school O.T.C., including one year as a cadet officer. He surrendered his Oxford Scholarship and what that might have meant in order to join up at once. He passed through the battalion from end to end, occupying at various times every possible place: signalling officer, intelligence officer, platoon commander, company commander, adjutant, 2nd in command . . . and when we add that he excelled in every position separately and distinctly, and won the admiration and love of all, we may spare him further embarrassment and let the honours he has won speak for him.

By the end of the War, Hills had won the Military Cross and Bar, the Croix de Guerre with bronze star and two Mentions in Despatches. His evident closeness to his commanding officer ('he excelled in every position . . . and won the admiration and love of all') disqualifies Hills as a completely disinterested analyst of how the Fifth Leicesters were led during the Great War. His style – stolid, formulaic, ruthlessly unemotional – reveals the qualities of a successful militarist. Hills accounts for every day that the Fifth Leicesters spent on active service, from their arrival at Le Havre on February 27th 1915 (each man was given a pair of socks as a welcome present from Queen Mary) to the declaration of the Armistice at the village of Sains du Nord on November 11th, 1918. For seekers after Walter Butterworth, Hills's qualifications are beyond doubt; he began his career as a subaltern in 'D' Company and was therefore certain to have known Walter by sight if not by name.

The Fifth Leicesters spent 637 days in trenches during the Great War. The other 717 days were taken up with marching, resting or training. The battalion went over the top in full strength on 12 separate occasions. Hills describes each one in sequential detail, and refers with similar exactitude to the football matches, athletic tournaments and shooting competitions that the Fifth Leicesters played against their brigade and divisional rivals in between battles. In all, Hills mentions by name 351 officers and other ranks, not counting an additional 79 men whose gallantry awards are listed in an appendix. Nowhere in 375 pages, including maps and photographs, does he mention Walter Butterworth. In order to qualify for recognition in the battalion history, a soldier of the Fifth Leicesters had to be: a) an officer; b) conspicuously brave; c) killed or badly wounded in a manner approved of by Captain J.D. Hills.

As a unit of a battalion, Walter was invisible. British General Headquarters didn't fight with battalions, it fought with divisions – twelve battalions grouped into three brigades. The Fifth Leicesters were part of the 138th Brigade (Lincs and Leics), which was one of the three brigades of the 46th (North Midland) Division. When the Fifth Leicesters finally took possession of the Western Front, it was a narrow strip of the sector assigned to the 46th Division, which took me to the hamlet of Wulverghem, south of Ypres.

In the words of David Lloyd George, the task facing Britain's part-time soldiers in early 1915 was to hold the sodden trenches of Flanders until the volunteers of Lord Kitchener's armies were ready to take the field. At Wulverghem, the sodden trenches were dominated so completely by the Germans – from the top of a hillock known as Spanbroekmoelen (Windmill Hill) – that hardly anyone moved on the British side during daylight. The British artillery was so short of ammunition that the batteries attached to the 46th Division were rationed to 20 rounds per gun per day. By the middle of May 1915, the allowance had dwindled to two rounds per gun per day.

The rotation of the two Lincoln and two Leicester battalions of 138th Brigade at Wulverghem was: four days in the front line; four days in support; four days in reserve. Each evening, if they were in support, the Leicesters gathered at one of the sector's derelict farms for a hot breakfast, followed by a tot of rum in their tea if they were lucky. As soon as it was fully dark they set off. On their first trip to the firing line the priority was ammunition and orders. Food went up in sandbags, each containing enough bread, tea, sugar, tobacco and tinned-stuffs for four men. Water was delivered in Shell and Pratt petrol tins holding two gallons each. The second trip up the line, and the third if there was time, was for trench materials such as wire, corrugated iron, stanchions, sandbags, planks. And chloride of lime for the corpses. When the rain churned everything to mud, it could take four hours to complete a round journey that measured less than two miles on the map.

The Leicesters' firing line, half-way up the German-held slope, consisted of isolated posts in excavated shell-holes and sandbag breastworks known as 'grouse butts'. All of them stank horribly, being partly constructed of dead bodies left over from the fighting of 1914. French and Belgian dead in red and blue uniforms mouldered in No Man's Land alongside bundles of khaki and field-grey. Bloated cattle and a team of dead horses still tethered to their limber rotted among the thistles and weeds. With practice, the Leicesters learned to differentiate the dead of separate species by smell alone. And into this foul sump the Germans on the higher ground spilt their own torrents of ordure and filth.

The Fifth Leicesters, like the conscientious Territorials they were, beavered away on the outline of a proper trench system. They had arrived at Wulverghem to find only one communication trench up to the front line, a filthy ditch called Piccadilly which flooded up to waist height every time it rained. When Piccadilly's sides collapsed, the nocturnal carrying parties were forced over the top and into harassing fire from the fixed rifles which the Germans had sighted on all the main British routes. It was dull, dangerous work. Walter was a pack beast by night and zombie by day. With each dawn, he and his comrades crept away to sleep, huddling in corners under greatcoats or ground-sheets. During their four days in the firing line they had no sleep at all. Nor was there much rest when the Lincolns and Leicesters were in 'Rest'. The officers could ride the few miles into Bailleul for a meal at the Hotel Faucon, or a drink at Tina's Café, or a bath in the semi-derelict asylum. No such civilising influences were available to the men. For the rank and file, 'Divisional Rest' meant musketry, drill, bomb-throwing practice (with tins of jam instead of grenades) and plenty of digging.

Most of the farms around Wulverghem, although roofless, were still recognisable as one-time habitations. Cookers Farm was closest to the Germans and therefore the most dangerous, followed by Frenchman's Farm, which housed Battalion HQ, and then Pond Farm, where half the reserve Company lived. Furthest back from the front line, on the road into Wulverghem proper, was the comparative safety of Packhorse Farm, which housed the Regimental Aid Post and billets for the remainder of the reserve Company. 'This last was also the burying ground for the sector,' says Hills, 'and the rendezvous for transport and working parties.'

Pond Farm was rebuilt after the War and made accessible to pilgrims by a track of awkward right-angles leading to an adjacent British cemetery, the wall surrounding which yielded an excellent view of the shallow valley in which the Lincolns and Leicesters had been dug in. I orientated myself with the aid of a trench map in

Peter Chasseaud's collection, 'Topography of Armageddon'. The knoll of Spanbroekmoelen to my left was marked by a tonsure of shrubs and trees; Cookers Farm was down to my right; Packhorse Farm was about equidistant to the rear.

The pond of Pond Farm was still there, gloomily green, surrounded by pollarded willows, home to a single moody swan. A farmyard dog barked at my approach but soon returned to his dusty patch of sunlight. The kitchen garden contained neat rows of beans and cabbages. No one stirred, except a man-sized scarecrow hanging by his neck from the beam of the barn door.

Walter had been through here, weighed down with gear, alert for any flash or bang from Spanbroekmoelen. He'd had callused hands and red eyes and mud in every crevice of his face. I imagined him as one of Wilfred Owen's men, bent-backed, knock-kneed, cursing through slime. 'There were grids to walk on,' says Hills, 'but the slabs had been placed longtitudinally on cross runners, and many of us used to slide off into some swampy hole.'

Some of them slid off for good. At Packhorse Farm, where the stretcher-bearers had lived, I found another little cemetery. Of more than 2,000 British graveyards on the Western Front this one was unique, containing only Leicesters and Lincolns, 27 of each, men of the 138th Brigade killed in the three months of April–May–June 1915. 'We lost about two killed and ten wounded each tour,' says Hills, 'mostly from snipers and stray bullets, for we did not come into actual conflict with the enemy at all.'

The Territorial Army was sneered at by the Regulars for being windy in battle and sluttish in trenches. The Minister for War, Lord Kitchener, conceded that the Terriers might be of some use for Home Defence, but their main use overseas was merely to plug gaps. The amateur officers of the 138th Brigade at Wulverghem worked their men hard. By the end of May a new trench called

Pall Mall had joined Piccadilly as an alternative route for forward communications. Both trenches had been drained and floored with duckboards, each had a squad of men assigned to permanent repair and maintenance. On May 28th 1915, the final work of beautification was completed when the rotten cows and stinking horses were dragged into a shell hole and cremated. Then, just as the Fifth Leicesters were beginning to feel at home, it was time to shift. As summer took hold and the weather improved – or grew less bad – the 46th Division was ordered into the Salient proper.

After the near-breakthrough at Neuve Chapelle, everyone had been expecting a bigger show at the next opportunity, and it was anticipated around Ypres because that was where the British were most under pressure. The Germans had attacked in April with that deadly novelty, poison gas. French and Algerian troops had panicked and fled. There was nothing between the Germans and the city of Ypres except the half-blind, half-choked survivors of broken regiments. Yet when they reached the limit of their own gas cloud the Germans hesitated and the Canadians rushed famously into the breach to hold the line.

In after years, when those who returned told of Ypres they conveyed the geography of the Salient by cupping their hands to describe a saucer. The city of Ypres lay at the saucer's flat centre; the Germans held the high ground around the lip; the British were in the middle, under fire from three sides. During the Great War, more than 1 million men of all nations were killed or wounded in the shallow amphitheatre of the Salient. Withdrawal to a flatter line, the sensible military course for the British, had been declared unthinkable. Ypres defended the vital supply lines through the Channel ports which sustained the British Army in the field. Ypres was where, after the retreat from Mons in 1914, the old Regular Army had made its stand and perished. Too much blood had been shed for Ypres to be abandoned; it would

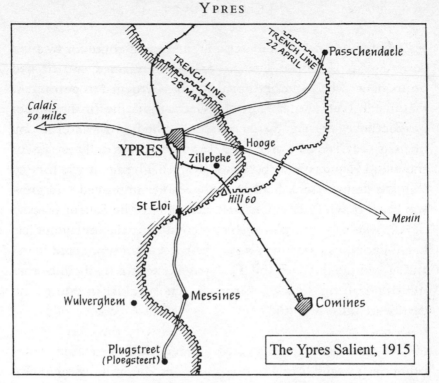

The Ypres Salient, 1915

have to be redeemed. The Germans would have to be pushed from the ridges. When the high ground had been cleared, the big punch would go in, opening the way for breakthrough. Beyond the German lines lay good galloping country. Big punch. Cavalry charge. Onward to Victory. Strategy in a nutshell.

The German gas attack of April 22nd changed all the plans. In the six weeks of fighting that followed, the area of British-held ground around Ypres shrank by about two-thirds. By the end of May, the German line of encirclement was less than three miles from the city itself. It became known as the Second Battle of Ypres. The British counted it as a stubborn (58,000 casualties) defence, the Germans as a missed (47,000 casualties) opportunity. Second Ypres was the baptism of fire of the Territorial Army.

The Fifth Leicesters marched north on July 1st 1915. As they approached the southern gate of Ypres, the Lille Gate, they turned right (Shrapnel Corner) and took an easterly route over the swampy flats towards Zillebeke Lake, a triangular reservoir which had been left wrecked and be-slimed by the German bombardment. Passing the lake, and dodging the German machine guns sighted on Zillebeke church, the Leicesters reached Maple Copse. By nightfall they were holding the line among the ghostly stumps of Sanctuary Wood, where they were strafed every couple of hours by whizz-bangs – so called because the bang of the shell exploding was heard only a split second after the whizz of it coming through the air. When the Fifth Leicesters were withdrawn to rest after their first tour of duty, Sanctuary Wood had cost them seven men killed and 26 wounded. When the time came to return, with the clothes still damp on their backs, they were sent to Hill 60, one of the deadliest contours on the map.

Hill 60 was barely as tall as a five-storey building. In any other landscape it would hardly have registered as a distinct topographical feature, being comprised mainly of the spoil from an adjacent railway cutting. In the flatlands of Flanders, however, Hill 60 offered unrivalled observation for miles around and the British and the Germans fought for it ceaselessly, using every means at their disposal. Wherever the opposing lines came close enough – and at Bomb Corner they were within throwing range – both sides burrowed towards each other with evil intent.

At 1900 hours, July 19th 1915, as the Fifth Leicesters ate their supper on Hill 60, the Royal Engineers blew up 1½ tons of explosive under the front-line hamlet of Hooge a couple of miles away. The cloud-scorching flash of the explosion was followed by a crashing wave of concussion, under cover of which a battalion of Middlesex stormed forth to occupy the resultant crater. Hooge and its château were totally obliterated in the fighting that followed. By the end of the War, it was a signpost in the middle of a vast crater field. But in 1920 the road to Menin slowly re-emerged, followed by the shanties of the first returning refugees. Later still a British cemetery was added, and a church. Today the road from Ypres to Menin runs broader and straighter and faster than ever, so fast that it's easy to pass through Hooge before recognising it.

First the Great War, then the pilgrims. Next came another war, followed by neglect. Then came tourism. Hooge's rebuilt château has been converted into a leisure complex and renamed Bellewaerde Park. Splash pools and water-chutes occupy the ground where British and German infantry clawed for possession. At the demure, chalet-style hotel I was invited to refresh myself with 'English Tea' before viewing, for a modest charge, the 'archaeological trench' that had been discovered in the garden:

> At a depth of just over two metres a section of duckboarding was discovered . . . As the trench was gradually uncovered more evidence came to light. Stronger, thicker timbers, sandbags, communication wires, rifles, bayonets, complete bundles of uniforms and hundreds of bullets were discovered. When the project was completed it was felt that, given the wealth of evidence unearthed, it was possible to restore the trench accurately to its original condition, providing a unique opportunity for a modern generation to see at first hand the details of trench life in a completely original setting.

The Middlesex stormed Hooge crater and tried to consolidate under a pulverising bombardment. The shelling was so intense that the 46th Division, as the next division in line, was asked to stage a diversion. Specifically, the Fifth Leicesters were ordered to distract German attention from Hooge by detonating two of the mines which the Royal Engineers had dug under the Germans on top of Hill 60.

At 1855 hours, July 23rd 1915, after a day of thunder and showers, the first mine was blown. The Germans responded by turning rifle fire on the Leicesters from all directions. Six minutes later the second, bigger mine exploded, sending the contents of a German redoubt high into the air along with huge clods of clay. Before the debris landed the British artillery had opened up, and for the next half-hour the Germans on Hill 60 were pasted with a cannonade of all calibres.

Retribution came at 2135 hours. Trench 50 went skyward without warning. Dazed and deafened Leicesters surfaced to find that their trench had been replaced by a reeking, fume-filled crater into which the Germans were already lobbing 'sausages' – fat, black mortar bombs stuffed with high explosive. As the wounded were pulled from the wreckage, survivors formed a firing line to hold the lip of the crater while new defences could be excavated.

The Leicesters dug and fought all night, and all the next day. They stayed an extra 24 hours beyond their scheduled relief in order to be able to hand over a properly traversed replacement for Trench 50 to the Lincolns. The cost of the tour was 40 killed, missing or wounded in 'B' Company, from the German mine, plus the usual score of casualties from routine wastage. It couldn't go on. Since Lieutenant Aked had got them off the mark, the Fifth Leicesters had been reduced to nearly half their strength. Nine Company officers remained available for trench duty, and 474 men. At this rate, the Fifth Leicesters would be extinct by the end of the year.

After the War, Hill 60 joined Hooge as one of the recognised way-stations of pilgrimage in The Salient. The long, straight, uphill road from Zillebeke village – the same road which once gave the German machine guns such a deadly field of fire – was tamed by traffic-calming measures for the better protection of suburban cyclists. The top of Hill 60, pitted with vestigial earthworks, was fenced off and signposted as a communal war grave:

> In the broken tunnels beneath this enclosure many British and German dead were buried and the hill is therefore preserved, so far as nature will permit, in the state in which it was left after the Great War.

With the passage of years, the lower slopes of Hill 60 disappeared under the chalet-style domestic architecture so popular in Belgium. In the shadow of a towering electricity-generating windmill, some visionary was breeding ostriches. The birds' anachronistic squawks followed me as I slid into the railway cutting which once had been a zone of certain death. Alongside the track lay Larch Wood Cemetery, partially obscured by a chance fold of ground from the top of Hill 60. This slight element of protection presumably explained why the British had selected the site for an Aid Post. If Uncle Peter was right, and if Walter had been blown up in a trench at Hill 60, this was where he would have been treated . . .

My mood of psycho-literary retrospection was broken by the arrival of a charabanc of firemen from Devon in full uniform. Like me, they were visiting Ypres to mark the anniversary of the Armistice. I had suspected that it might be a busy time of year. In 1925, when the writer Henry Williamson made the same pilgrimage, he estimated that Hill 60 was attracting 10,000 visitors a week. In those days the going rate for souvenirs ranged from 50 centimes for a brass button up to 20 francs for a Smith & Wesson revolver.

The Queen Victoria Rifles Café atop Hill 60 was heaving with Devonshire firemen when I arrived. I withdrew with my bottle of Euro-lager to examine some of the trophies that had been recovered from the surrounding fields. Amongst the tarnished heraldry on display I found three cap badges of the Leicestershire Regiment – three grinning tigers under the Imperial motto, 'Hindoostan'. The Fifth Leicesters had paid a heavy price to hold Trench 50 and some of them held it still:

> Before we left [says Hills], we found Serjeant Bunn's body; he had been buried at his post, and was still holding in his hand the flare pistol which he was going to fire when the mine exploded. The men of the listening post were not found until some time later, for they had been thrown several hundred yards by the explosion.

On July 30th 1915, the Germans attacked Hooge again with torrents of liquid fire. As with the gas attack in April, the use of a new weapon against an unprepared enemy had a devastating effect. Those who fell prostrate in their trenches stood a chance of survival as the burning vapour whooshed noisily, but harmlessly, overhead. Those who tried to escape, the majority, were incinerated. The Germans punched through the British lines as far as Zouave Wood, and once again the way to Ypres was open. Two British battalions, the 9th Kings Royal Rifles and 9th Rifle Brigade, were thrown into an improvised counter-attack. They'd marched eight miles out to rest before being ordered straight back again. The Fifth Leicesters watched from Sanctuary Wood as the riflemen tried to charge uphill only to be wiped out almost to a man.

The Leicesters were told to stand by for the next attempt. They spent a night and a day without cover in Maple Copse, cowering under the fire pouring down from Zouave Wood. At the last minute, instead of attempting another doomed attack uphill, Hills says the Leicesters were ordered to dig a new communication trench:

At dawn on the 3rd, there was a trench the whole way [to Zillebeke], not very deep in places and not perhaps very scientifically dug, but still enough to give cover. As soon as work was over we returned to the copse and slept, for at dusk that night we were to go once more to the line and relieve the Lincolnshires.

Zouave Wood was so comprehensively eradicated by the War that it was never replanted. Maple Copse was renewed, but askew from its original site. Part of it became Maple Copse Cemetery from where, by lining up with the rebuilt tower of Zillebeke church, I was able to imagine the route of the communication trench which had cost the Leicesters 35 men killed or wounded on August Bank Holiday, 1915.

The Fifth Leicesters spent two months trudging the sidelines of the on-off slogging match known as the battle for Hooge. Tours of duty at Sanctuary Wood and Hill 60 were interspersed with spells of rest in the scruffy hutments of Ouderdom and Locre, villages behind the lines where the Leicesters marched, trained and diverted themselves with bloodthirsty games of football. As autumn drew on the Leicesters readied themselves, along with the rest of the British Expeditionary Force, for the final effort of 1915. Lingering French doubts about the military commitment of the British were to be laid to rest by a series of co-ordinated actions along the length of the Western Front. Two big French thrusts would be directed against the Germans in Artois and Champagne, while the British helped out with a large-scale diversion at Loos. To further distract the Germans and pin down their reserves, there would be smaller British attacks in Flanders. The Leicesters and Lincolns of 138th Brigade were told to confuse the Germans with a dummy gas cloud while yet another attack was launched against Hooge.

At dawn on September 25th 1915, as the British took the offensive on the Western Front, the Fifth Leicesters at Sanctuary Wood stood ready with their boxes of matches and, at the given order, mounted the firestep to light the damp straw they'd spread on their parapets the night before. The neighbouring battalion of Staffords did not, with the result that the Germans – thinking indeed that they were being attacked with gas – concentrated all their firepower on the Leicesters. By the time the Germans realised that the smoke was a ploy, it had cost the Leicesters 42 men killed or wounded. The cost in Staffords was not computed.

The cost of entry to the Sanctuary Wood Trench Museum was 100 Belgian francs . . .

Some of Sanctuary Wood's original trees have survived. Each blackened trunk, rotted to the fibrous consistency of balsa, is stigmatised with bullet holes. I touched them, Thomas-like, with doubtful finger-tips. The Museum's trenches, vestiges of the real-life Vince Street and Jam Row, looked false because they had been maintained in textbook trim over many years. But they were indisputably genuine, at least in the sense that they were still roughly in the same place where they had been photo-graphed in 1919. Now British schoolboys charged up and down making staccato machine-gun noises at the backs of their throats: 'Uh-uh-uh-uh-uh-uh-uh-oof. Fuck you, Parry, you're dead!'

It was impossible to know for sure if Walter had ever been in Vince Street, although Lincolns and Leicesters were certainly regu-lar visitors. According to the diary of Captain Robert Fieldsend, machine-gun officer of the Fourth Lincolns, the 138th Brigade had been deployed further up the slope and to the right at Zero hour:

At 4.50 a.m. we lighted the straw to deceive the enemy
and opened rapid rifle and machine-gun fire as the 14th

and 3rd Divisions attacked and took the enemy's trenches [at Hooge], where our artillery fire had been concentrated . . . During all this we had to be on a constant look-out for the enemy's counter-attacks, and while observing for a favourable machine-gun target at 6.15 a.m. I was struck on the left side of my face by a bullet.

After the first shock of the blow, which knocked me right over, I felt no pain but could feel that I was losing a great deal of blood. I was quite conscious of everything and could hear what everybody said but could see nothing. Sergeant Drewry bound me up and I was carried on a stretcher to the 'Advanced Aid Post' about 500 yards away in the Railway Cutting just below Hill 60 [Larch Wood] . . . The Medical Officer had a look at me and gave me an injection of morphia. After I had been there half an hour, I was carried on a stretcher to the Railway Dug-outs and from there on a wheeled stretcher to Kruistraat . . . I again received a hypodermic injection, this time as a preventative against lockjaw . . . I was put on a motor ambulance and taken to No. 10 Casualty Clearing Station near Poperinghe. Here, I just remember being given an anaesthetic and I was then stitched up and my left eye removed.

I walked up Vince Street, ducking schoolboys' imaginary bullets, until it stopped abruptly at a fence. Looking out, I realised that it was not the trench that felt spurious but the surrounding farms, fields and hedgerows. The present tense was out of place in this landscape. I wanted to follow Vince Street all the way to that muddy dugout under Hill 60, where Walter and his section might yet be sitting out the bombardment. The green fields of peace and prosperity seemed no more substantial to me than a stage painting; behind it, if only I could pierce the veil, was the reality of the Great War I yearned for.

The 20-year-old Edmund Blunden had walked up Vince Street, mentioning it by name in *Undertones of War*. Standing to watch British field guns firing in Maple Copse, Blunden had looked down and found a buckled British helmet at his feet, still plastered with blood and hair. Sanctuary Wood Cemetery contains the graves of nearly 2,000 British dead, including eight of the Leicesters blown up by the mine on Hill 60:

Biddle. Buswell. Hall. Ibbotson.
Pennington. Pick. Randall. Simpson.

And with them Sergeant A.C. Bunn,
killed at his post, July 23rd 1915.

Leicesters buried among Lincolns, for the sake of Hill 60.

Winston Churchill wanted to leave Ypres in ruins after the War so that it might serve, like Pompeii, as a permanent reminder of the beastliness which had fallen upon it. Instead, it became a monument to the tenacity of the Belgian bourgeoisie. Stone by stone, the people of Ypres rebuilt their town in the image of how it had been. They rescued their streets from under the rubble, replicated the houses, replanted the gardens. Season by season, the battlefields were tilled, harrowed flat and restored to health. Children went back to school, church bells rang. Peace unrolled like a prayer mat, squashing the dark secrets of the Salient deeper and deeper underground. Hellblast Corner became a roundabout.

Ypres' restored Cloth Hall is undoubtedly a fine achievement, if you like pseudo-medieval architecture built out of Lego bricks. I found myself siding with Churchill. There was a faint hint of complacency about restored Ypres. I could not stand in front of the Cloth Hall or the Cathedral without seeing through them to the stupendous, admonitory ruins they once had been. Anyone can build a city, any city made perfect. It was the flames I was interested in, not the phoenix which had risen from the ashes.

The only place in Ypres where I was able to catch a plausible hint of the Great War was the ramparts. At dusk at the Lille Gate I thought I caught the sound of battle – alarums, orders, men in strife – but it was only a trick of the sound waves bouncing across from a game of football on the other side of the moat. Night settled like gauze upon the topmost branches of the poplars. Edmund Blunden had served nearby, in a brick vault commandeered as a Brigade HQ. It was impossible to think about the War without remembering the poetry which had first revealed it to me:

> . . . We stood, hard-watching in the eastward dark,
> A glowing pyre and vapour by Hill Sixty,
> And wondered who was mocking, Peace or War?
> The last train answered with far-dying echoes,
> And passed along the cutting; now the plain
> Lay in its first sleep, and all its dwellings slept . . .

There was noise and bustle in the café, and lots of light. Belgians raised their foaming tankards and stabbed vigorously at platters of ham and chips. Behind the laughter, I tried to listen for the sinister murmur I had heard so many times before. I had come to touch the War; now the War touched me in the person of Joe Fitzpatrick. His twin sister was christened Mary. Joseph and Mary were born on Christmas Day 1895, to good Catholic folk. Joe joined the Manchesters and marched through the Menin Gate.

'Shut that door!'

Somebody brought Joe Fitzpatrick into t'Sverde restaurant, parked him at a table and went out again into the frosty night to move the car. I glanced up from my ham and chips and knew instantly that I was looking at a veteran. Joe's eyes, marbled with great age, were turned in upon himself. His skin was dry, but there was strength in his handshake. He held me by the wrist while he talked. I wanted to ask him the questions I might have asked Walter. What was it like? Was your sergeant a bastard? How many Germans did you kill for sure? Who were your friends? Where did they die? Did you shit yourself going over the top? Did you funk it, let your mates down? What was the worst?

Medals jingled under Joe's overcoat as he brought out his wallet and unwrapped a wad of newspaper clippings. Signed up May 5th 1915, 2nd/6th Manchesters. Served at Nieupoort, Passchendaele, Cambrai. Captured March 1918.

'This German officer stuck his revolver in my stomach and said, "You come." Well, that were the end of my War.'

Joe told me the story he had told five hundred times before. He didn't remember the War; he was too old. What Joe remembered were stories about the War that he'd told before.

'You like football?' he asked, introducing his pet subject. 'What's your team?'

I was born in the shadow of Filbert Street. 'Leicester City,' I said.

Joe snatched up my wrist with renewed enthusiasm.

'Do you know what they were called,' he said, 'before the War? Leicester Fosse, that's what.'

The Great War was the grave of Leicester Fosse. Their final home game at Filbert Street was a 5-nil stuffing of Leeds. Their final game ever – after the War, Fosse were reconstituted as Leicester City – was a 2-nil defeat at Clapton Orient on April 24th 1915. The programme for that match shows a squad of fans in uniform marching out of the ground behind an officer. A sign on a gas lamp points to 'The Front' while a recruiting sergeant beckons the reader: 'Come, all ye slackers; fall in behind! Your last chance for the Berlin Final.'

Walter and his comrades in the 46th Division were prime specimens of the type. Improvised goal-posts sprouted around their billets as soon as they came out of the line. Hills says that one officer in every battalion, usually the Padre, was permanently designated 'O-i-C, Football':

Our [Christmas] celebrations included a Brigade Cup competition for which we entered a hot side, including many of our old players – 'Banger' Neal, 'Mush' Taylor, Toon, Archer, Skelly, Fish, Sargeant Allan, Kirchin, and others. We met the 5th Lincolnshires in the semi-finals and beat them 2–1, and then turned our attention to their 4th battalion, who after beating our 4th battalion, our old rivals, met us in the final and went down 1–0. The final was a keen, hard game, played well to the finish, and we deserved our win. The trophy – a clock, mounted in a French '75' shell – was taken back to Leicestershire by Captain Farmer when he next went on leave.

'Football!?' says Uncle Peter. 'Did Walter play football? He were mad about it. He were at Filbert Street the Saturday afore he died – him, me and your Uncle Mick. We won three-one against Rotherham. Rowley scored a penalty. Top goal-scorer in history, Arthur Rowley, and he never played for England. Used to make your grandad mad, that did.'

On November 11th, Remembrance Sunday, I joined Ypres' annual salute to 'The Glorious Dead'. A British ambassador and a British general led worship in the church of St George, which was followed by a procession to the Menin Gate, the vaulted archway in Ypres' eastern ramparts on which are carved the names of nearly 55,000 British soldiers who marched into the Salient but to whom the fortunes of war denied the known and honoured burial given to their comrades in death. As Kipling put it. A stone catafalque crowned the archway facing the town; an imperial lion guarded the approaches. There was plenty of time, while we spectators waited for the dignitaries, to admire the Menin Gate's Doric simplicity. Children from local schools fidgeted. The British Armed Forces were represented by plump squaddies of both sexes. There was no military band, just some trumpet-playing firemen from Devon.

At the sacred moment – the eleventh hour of the eleventh day of the eleventh month – nothing happened. The tail-end of the procession from St George's was still slouching down Meensestraat.

At the thirty-second minute of the eleventh hour of the eleventh day, the 'Last Post' sounded. Joe Fitzpatrick and his fellow veterans shuffled forward to lay their wreaths of poppies. A choir crooned dirges. The ambassador and the general laid their wreaths, followed by the widows and orphans of later wars.

At the fifty-seventh minute of the eleventh hour of the eleventh day, the two-minute silence fell. Paper petals cascaded down and drifted in crimson swathes across the cobbles. I was not wearing my poppy; it had fallen off on my first night in town and I had not replaced it. Ypres was swarming with poppy-blazoned Britishers and, perversely, I didn't want to be associated with them. I was reluctant to share my personal obsession with the Great War, presumably because I balked at recognising myself. In London, I had worn my poppy with pride; in Ypres, it felt ostentatious.

The ceremony of remembrance played itself out with a disappointing lack of conviction. The well-fed squaddies were unsure of what they were meant to be doing. The poem chosen for recitation was a girlish imitation of a Great War poem:

> Do not stand at my grave and weep,
> I am not there, I do not sleep,
> I am a thousand winds that blow,
> I am the diamond glints on snow . . .
>
> (Anon)

I listened with a smouldering sense of outrage. Where was the pride? What was the purpose? The fat-arsed squaddies couldn't march! The whole ceremony had been organised to emphasise the waste and futility of war in general rather than to celebrate the Great War's specific, poignant radiance. None spoke of Honour or Justice, or what it had cost to defend these virtues in 1914. The British spectators seemed anxious to avoid any explicit approbation of their ancestral triumph – as if their foremost duty, as good citizens of Europe, was to forgive and forget. Which was impossible if, like me, every day of your life was Remembrance Day. I left the Menin Gate and hurried to the battlefield of Loos while there was still daylight left.

Captain J.D. Hills of the Fifth Leicesters was my *vade mecum* to the Western Front, but I had found another travelling companion in the shape of Captain John Milne, whose book *Footprints of the Fourth Leicestershires* was everything that Hills' was not. Hills only felt comfortable with his emotions when expressing anger or disapproval, and most of his attempted jokes turned out to be duds. The conscientiously unambitious nature of his prose style is amply demonstrated in his account of the German mine explosion at Hill 60:

39

Before the debris had stopped falling, Captain Griffiths [commander of 'B' Company] was out of his dug-out and scrambling along his half filled trench to find out what had happened. Reaching the right end of '50' he found his front line had been completely destroyed, and where his listening post had been was now a large crater . . . Except for a few wounded men, he could see nothing of Serjt. Bunn and the garrison of the trench, most of whom he soon realized must have been buried, where the tip of the crater had engulfed what had been the front line . . . Nor had he sufficient men in the left of his trench to bring across to help the right, so, sending down a report of his condition, he started, with any orderlies and batmen he could collect, to rescue those of his company who had been only partially buried. Meanwhile help was coming . . . On the right, Colonel Martin, of the 4th Battalion, also disturbed at dinner, was soon up in '49' trench, where he found that his left flank had also suffered from the explosion, but not so badly.

Hills' main concern is to justify the actions of a brother-officer in dealing with the professional problem of having his forward position blown away without warning during dinner. Lay readers are given no clues as to what the experience might have felt like because Hills is uninterested in personal themes. Years of being sneered at by Regulars had left their mark. Hills' motive in writing was refutation. He wanted to prove that, man for man, the Territorials in general and the Fifth Leicesters in particular could be as hard, as brave, as soldierly as any battalion of Regulars.

Compare Hills' methods with those of Captain Milne:

After the explosion, trench 50 was just one-half acre of agony. Men were literally buried in heaps, one on top of the other, all mixed up with sandbags, beams of dug-outs, corrugated iron, machine guns, rum jars and ammunition boxes. Arms and legs protruded from the debris, and cries and groans came from crumpled and broken heaps of humanity ejaculating, 'Oh, Jesus,' and 'For Christ's sake, get me out,' half in imprecation, half in prayer. The 4th and 5th worked furiously to unearth the buried men. It was not an easy job because of the darkness and the difficulty of removing beams and debris from the top of men lest they should fall on others underneath. Shells were passing overhead, and our men on each side of trench 50 fired 'rapid'. The M.O. of the 5th (M.H. Barton) worked like a Trojan getting the wounded out.

Writing twenty years after the event, in 1935, Milne is still able to hear the cries of the wounded. When he shuts his eyes, he can still see their mangled bodies. As sister battalions in the same brigade, the Fourth Leicesters and the Fifth Leicesters fought side by side throughout the War. They defended the same trenches, muddied the same billets, buried their dead beside each other. When one battalion suffered disproportionate casualties, it was strengthened by transfusions of manpower from the other. Hills was to be my prime source because he provided the dates, times and locations necessary to follow Walter and 'D' Company in battle. But Hills on his own was not enough. Hills worked in monochrome, Milne conveyed light and shade. Hills was factual, Milne was truthful. Hills reports that when their time in The Salient came to an end, the Leicesters entrained at the village of Abeele at 1530 hours, October 2nd 1915. Milne records what the men sang as they marched:

> *We are the Leicester Boys,*
> *We are the Leicester Boys.*
> *We know our manners,*

We spend our tanners,
We are respected wherever we go.

When you see us on parade,
Open the windows wide.
All the girls begin to cry,
'I tiddly, I tiddly, I ti, ti.'
We are the Leicester Boys.

A British division on the march swallowed up 15 miles of narrow French road: 12,000 men, 6,000 horses, heavy and light artillery, ammunition limbers, supply waggons, ambulances, field kitchens, mobile repair workshops, sanitation units . . . At regulation speed and spacing – seven steps between platoons and ten minutes rest each hour – it would have taken the 46th Division five hours to pass any given spot. Which is why most of them went south in instalments, on the divisional train.

The Leicesters had a pretty good idea of their eventual destination, but they blotted it out with songs and cigarettes and endless games of cards. When the train stopped inexplicably, as troop trains always did, they jumped down from their cattle trucks and went looking for something edible to scrounge. They were heading for Loos. Liddell-Hart, in his *History of the First World War*, calls it the battle that nobody wanted. Most subsequent accounts begin with his caveat: the British were against Loos from the start, blame the French. It was the French Supremo, General Joffre, who proposed that the climactic Allied offensive of 1915 should consist of a two-pronged stab in Champagne and Artois, and it was General Joffre who ordained that the Artois thrust would combine a French assault at Vimy Ridge with a British one at Loos.

The commander entrusted with the British attack was Sir Douglas Haig, who toured the proposed battlefield and disliked it immediately. The plain north of Loos was a pancake-flat, coal-mining district with the Germans firmly dug in around numerous pit-heads and slag-heaps. The British would be attacking strongly fortified positions over exposed ground. When Haig protested that he didn't have the guns, or the ammunition, or the trained men to do the job justice, he was told by his political and military superiors to support the French as best he could and attack when it suited them.

Haig's Staff gave him two options. If the wind was in the right direction at Zero, he could advance behind a curtain of gas with six divisions on a wide front. If the wind was unhelpful at Zero, he could dispense with gas and attack with two divisions on a narrow front. In conformity with Joffre's overall plan, the aim was to breach the German lines north of Loos and bring in reserves to exploit the gaps. The ultimate strategic objective was the city of Lille, 12 miles behind the Germans' line and their main railway centre for northern France.

Zero was set for 0550 hours, Saturday, September 25th 1915. At that moment – while Walter and the Fifth Leicesters were lighting their damp straw at Sanctuary Wood – chlorine gas was released from thousands of canisters along a five-mile stretch of the British Line north of Loos. The wind was weak and contrary, in places it blew the gas back in men's faces. One division, the 15th, burst into the German lines and captured the small town of Loos, but the two divisions in reserve were held too far back to exploit the gap. They reached the Front after an exhausting march, a full 12 hours after Loos had been taken. They were Kitchener volunteers, novices in battle. When they were hit by German artillery and machine-gun fire they reeled back in confusion. In the end, a potential breakthrough was only saved from turning into a rout when the Guards arrived to stiffen the line.

The most vivid account of the battle, if not the most historically accurate, is that provided by Robert Graves, who served as a subaltern in the 2nd Royal Welsh Fusiliers. In *Goodbye To All That* Graves tells how senior commanders ignored warnings about the wind and gassed their own men for the sake of keeping to the timetable. He says the British artillery barrage was a puny affair. British communications were severed within minutes and, with many junior officers knocked out, the men were left without clear orders. Graves says his Colonel scarpered with a slight wound, and in the resulting vacuum of command nobody had a clue what was going on: '"What's happened? What's happened?" I asked. "Bloody balls-up," was the most detailed answer I could get.'

As the dust of battle settled, the British saw that although they had taken chunks out of the German line, several strongpoints remained in enemy hands. One in particular, the Hohenzollern Redoubt, was to become notorious. It was a knot of deeply dug trenches, fortified with machine-gun emplacements, bulging into the British line a few miles north of Loos. The Redoubt was covered from behind by the workings of a coal mine and a slag-heap known as Fosse 8. From the left it was covered by a nest of machine guns known as Mad Point. The Hohenzollern had been briefly captured and lost by the British on September 25th, and again on the 29th. Haig's trench maps showed it as a formidable threat; machine guns on top of Fosse 8 could reach anything on the plain beneath. A small lodgement in the outer trench of the Hohenzollern Redoubt had remained in British hands from earlier in the battle, but Haig wanted the whole of Fosse 8 nipped out before winter. It was for a third attempt at this excision that the 46th Division had been ordered south.

The Fifth Leicesters went by rail, via Béthune. I followed them by road, via Bailleul. A pause in the town's market square did not disclose the Hotel Faucon, nor a café called Tina's packed with champagne-quaffing subalterns. In the days when it had been the 46th Division's favourite rest billet, Bailleul had been a lace-making centre. Its merchants' houses had worn Baroque or Gothic façades, and there'd been an elaborate sundial on the old town hall. I loaded up on *frites* from a mobile *friterie* and ate them on a bench in front of a ruined church, the charred stump of which had been left in the municipal car park as a solitary reminder of the German advance of 1918, in which the old Bailleul had been scoured from the map. The afternoon sun was at its height by the time I reached Vermelles, the straggling post-industrial village which had once constituted the forward command post for the 46th Division's operation against the Hohenzollern Redoubt.

George Coppard, in his book *With A Machine Gun To Cambrai*, recalls that the ruined brewery of Vermelles was built over deep vaults whose warmth and comfort sheltered 'many uproarious games of Brag, Pontoon and Crown and Anchor'. Robert Graves was billeted in the village and describes harvesting redcurrants in its lush, neglected gardens. He played a cricket match in which a bird-cage, with a dead parrot still inside, formed the wicket. The ground around Vermelles was chalk. The trenches were deep and their grey walls, where they hadn't been revetted, were as sticky as glue. Peering through their periscopes, the first thing the Leicesters saw on arrival were tidy rows of British dead from September's assaults, including many Jocks with their kilts agley and their white arses sadly exposed. The second thing they saw was how completely the slag-heap of Fosse 8 dominated the battlefield. It was not, as Hills put it, a 'very encouraging' sight.

The Leicesters spent the next few days behind the lines at the village of Hesdigneul, preparing for their attack in detail. Anyone from Leicestershire would have felt immediately at home. Hesdigneul's stone church, its walled manor house, its patchwork of surrounding woods and fields all offered a recognisably feudal reflection of the English shires. As the only customer in Hesdigneul's only café, it was easy for me to imagine the Fifth Leicesters setting up their tents on the broad village green. I could almost hear the boots as 'D' Company wheeled and turned on the square of communal gravel now set aside for games of *boules*.

The day after arriving in Hesdigneul, selected NCOs were bussed up to Vermelles to see the front line for themselves. That small part of the Hohenzollern Redoubt which had remained in British hands, a length of the trench known as Big Willie, had been defended against German counter-moves by skilful use of the Mills bomb. Divisional Staff seized on the idea that the Mills bomb, with its longer range than previous types of hand-grenade, was the tactical weapon to unlock the Hohenzollern's deep trenches and solid dugouts. The Divisional Commander, Major-General Montagu-Stuart-Wortley, thought that the best course was to bomb from trench to trench until the whole position had been captured.

A model of the trenches of the Hohenzollern Redoubt was improvised in a field near the château at Hesdigneul which had been commandeered as Brigade HQ. Here, the Leicesters practised throwing Mills bombs and were shown by the Royal Engineers how to 'reverse' German trenches once they had been captured. At a conference of Commanding Officers, Lieutenant-Colonel Jones was given the additional assurance that the Leicesters would be attacking behind the biggest artillery concentration of the War, comprising 54 heavy howitzers, 86 field howitzers and 286 field guns. General Haking, the Corps Commander, said the artillery and gas preparation would be so thorough that the infantry would advance against little or no opposition. As the final clincher, an extra element of surprise had been worked into the scheme – the Germans had grown so accustomed to dawn attacks that this time the British would go in after lunch. Otherwise it was the same battle plan as three weeks previously. Gas and artillery. Infantry charge. Onward to Victory. Strategy in a numbskull.

The Fourth and Fifth Leicesters paraded for battle on October 11th. They moved into the line the next day and took over from the Guards in fighting order. Their ammunition pouches were full (200 rounds per man), their greatcoats were rolled and strapped to their backs. The Brigadier managed to find them a band for part of the way, and the Fourth Leicesters, who were to form the first wave over the top, were in the front line by midnight. The Fifth Leicesters, assigned to support, were not brought into position until six hours later. Every man, as he passed the dumps in Vermelles, was given six extra sandbags. Every third man was given a shovel. Some were given wire-cutters and thick hedge gloves to deal with any German barbed wire that hadn't been uprooted by the artillery.

All through the following morning the Leicesters waited, packed so tightly into their trenches that they were unable to sit down. All Walter could see was the back of the neck of the man in front. Some managed to sleep standing up, until the British artillery opened at 1200 hours. Hills says it was a terrific bombardment and 'very encouraging'. Milne, watching from Vermelles, thought the guns were giving short measure: 'Surely this was not what had been promised?'

At 1300 hours the taps were turned on and clouds of chlorine gas drifted uncertainly towards the German lines. Rum was issued in the British trenches – dark, strong, Jamaica rum, the tradition being a double measure before an attack. As the final minutes ticked by, the Leicesters shook hands and peed for the last time.

They slapped each other on the back and swore encouragingly, each according to temperament.

'O Lord, thou knowest how busy I must be this day; if I forget thee, do not thou forget me.'

Men checked their gas-masks and then checked again, for one last time, the catches and clips they'd already checked fifty times before. Damn these bastard gas-masks, you couldn't breathe a drop. Calm down. Stop fussing.

Minutes turned to seconds. The corporals stood by the ladders. The officers put their whistles to their lips.

All the hills and vales along, the earth was bursting into song on the route of Walter's march to the Hohenzollern Redoubt. I shouted misremembered snatches of verse along the ribbon of road – Hesdigneul, Vaudricourt, Verquin – that had taken the Fifth Leicesters to Fosse 8, the actual road which had borne Walter into battle. I inhaled with relish the earthy vapours off the self-same autumn fields that he'd sniffed. I shouted the omens, headlines, poems, football chants: 'Come on you Leicesters! Come on you b-o-oys!!'

The Fifth Leicesters were pumped-up and primed for the fight. At Hesdigneul, Colonel Jones had called them together to remind them what they were fighting for: the safety of their families; the honour of their country; the pride of their regiment, the 17th Regiment of Foot, the Leicestershire Regiment. The Leicesters had won their first battle honour in 1695, with the capture of Namur under King William III. They had occupied New York during the American War of Independence and had kicked George Washington's arse at Princetown. In the Crimea, Sergeant Philip Smith had won one of the first Victoria Crosses ever awarded. The Leicestershire Regiment had defended Afghanistan, pacified India and captured Burma for the British Empire. Now it was Germany's turn. Let there be no mistake: the Leicesters had been ordered to take the Hohenzollern Redoubt, and take it they would.

At Verquin, the band of the Staffords led the march. At Sailly Labourse, the Major-General took the salute. At Vermelles, I parked the car and put on my wellington boots.

At 1350 hours, October 13th 1915, the gas cloud was turned off in the British trenches in front of the Hohenzollern Redoubt.

At 1355 hours the German machine guns opened up to check the range of the British lines.

At 1400 hours the whistles blew and the first waves of British infantry scrambled up their ladders.

The British parapets were thick with casualties within seconds. The wounded fell back on those trying to get out. Some made it into No Man's Land and attempted to form up in companies. The Fourth Leicesters lined up, one pace apart, and tried to advance in platoon order. Observers in Vermelles saw them picking their way clumsily over the tartan dreck left rotting after September's doomed charge. As the Leicesters bobbed towards the German wire, the machine-gunners at Mad Point blazed away with practised efficiency, hosing the churned-up ground in front of the Hohenzollern with a torrent of bullets. The first attackers to reach the Redoubt found that their wire-cutters were useless. The Germans had put up thick, ungalvanised steel wire, criss-crossed on stout posts and pit-props. In places it was 4 ft high and 20 ft across; there were some gaps, but not enough of them. The Fourth Leicesters were massacred as they searched desperately for the paths through the wire which their officers had promised them.

Throughout it all, the machine guns on Fosse 8 slag-heap reaped the support waves in methodical swathes. Of each line of men that set off for the Redoubt, barely a handful survived to jump into Big Willie or Little Willie trenches. And still the attack went on. The last of the Fourth Leicesters went over, followed by the

Fifth Lincolns, followed by the First Monmouths (138th Brigade Pioneers). The Fifth Leicesters moved up from support and sent forward signallers to lay a telephone cable.

The messages that came back were all bad. The leading battalions had entered the German front line but were encountering fierce opposition as they tried to move ahead. Instead of bombing their way forward as they had originally planned to do, the 46th Division had been ordered to storm the whole of Fosse 8 and capture its workings in one surge. The Leicesters were carrying out their side of the bargain, but the Staffords on the right had been chopped down at the knees. They'd started their advance from the support trenches but had got no further than their own front line. Without the Staffords to provide a right flank, it was suicide for the Leicesters and Lincolns to press on.

The messages from the Hohenzollern grew more urgent. More bombs; all officers killed; more bombs. The walking wounded and the hopelessly befuddled were beginning to straggle back. Brigade HQ, fearing a general retirement, told the Fifth Leicesters to do something quickly. For the first time in real life, Colonel Jones ordered his men into combat.

'B' Company climbed out of their support trench and formed ranks. The four platoon commanders were hit immediately. By the time 'B' Company reached the front line, where they jumped over Walter and the rest of 'D' Company, Captain Langdale was leading his men himself, with a pipe in his mouth. As they passed over he called out, 'Keep it up, Oakham!' to the platoon on his right. They were his last words. The men of Rutland went down like skittles, and Captain Langdale had his dottle knocked out for ever.

'A' Company followed, led by Captain Hastings. He kept his men bunched and charged the Germans with fixed bayonets. Some got into the Redoubt but were unable to advance. The trenches were full of dead and wounded men tangled together. Tactics, plans and objectives were abandoned. The outcome of individual combats failed to secure co-ordinated progress. Lieutenant Wollaston bombed his way up 80 yards of Little Willie trench before he ran out of grenades and had to retire.

With his men inside the Redoubt, their reinforcement and supply became Colonel Jones' immediate priority. He split 'D' Company into two. Platoons 13 and 14 were sent forward with a squad of sappers to lay barbed wire and help the Monmouths consolidate those parts of the Redoubt which could be strengthened. Hills says that even before they'd crossed the Leicesters' front line all the sappers had been killed. Those men of 'D' Company who survived formed themselves into bombing parties and headed for the Redoubt.

By 1700 hours, after three hours of fighting, the total extent of the 46th Division's advance amounted to a chunk of the Redoubt around Big Willie trench and a short length of the original German front line. As the German counter-attacks gathered strength, a rabble of various units pulled themselves together for a last stand. 'D' Company formed carrying parties to keep the fighting line supplied with bombs and ammunition from Vermelles.

The line held, partly by fluke. The strongest German counter-attack of the night came as a party of Sherwood Foresters advanced over the top to relieve the Leicesters. The Germans, mistaking the size of the reinforcements in the gloom, retired. Everybody knew it was a miserable achievement for such a concerted effort. The cost in Fifth Leicesters had been 26 officers and men killed; 13 missing; 156 wounded or gassed. The cost in Fourth Leicesters was almost unbelievable. They had led the assault against that section of the Hohenzollern Redoubt closest to the British line. Twenty officers – every one who had gone into battle – had been killed or wounded, and 453 other ranks. When roll-call was taken in Lancashire Trench on the way out, the Fourth Leicesters consisted of 188 NCOs and men.

Everyone knew why the attack had failed. The artillery hadn't destroyed Mad Point or the machine guns on the Fosse 8 slag-heap. Every man trying to reach the Hohenzollern Redoubt had been exposed to continuous machine-gun fire in enfilade without cover. And the gas had been a mistake. As soon as the Germans saw it, they knew an attack was coming. October 13th was a perfect day for gas according to the experts – bright and clear, with a wind from the south-west blowing at five miles per hour. Yet most of the chlorine settled in the craters of No Man's Land or dissipated before it got near the German lines. While it did virtually no harm to the Germans, it severely impeded the British, who were obliged to attack half-blinded and half-choked in their cumbersome gas-masks. Staff work and Intelligence had also been faulty; two trenches which had been identified as empty turned out to be full of Germans.

And then there were the bombs. The Leicesters had been promised Mills bombs, and Mills bombs only. At Hesdigneul they had practised on Mills bombs and Mills bombs only. But when they found themselves under attack at close quarters in the Hohenzollern Redoubt, fighting for their lives with the Mills bomb their only salvation, the Leicesters discovered that they'd been given different bombs, some of which they didn't even recognise. Worse, the few boxes of Mills bombs that did arrive – carried from Vermelles across No Man's Land by 'D' Company – were found to be duds, sent up without detonators. 'There can be no possible excuse for sending grenades into a fight without detonators,' says Hills, 'and no punishment could be too harsh for the officer who was responsible.'

For the survivors of the Fourth Leicesters there was no consolation in recrimination. The regiment had ceased to exist. Milne says that the two officers left behind on the day of the attack, of whom he must have been one, messed alone on the night of October 15th, 'and dared not look at each other'.

Robert Graves was drinking champagne cocktails in the Globe Café, Béthune, at lunchtime on October 13th 1915. He was loitering with a few friends on the off-chance of meeting the Prince of Wales, whose favourite watering hole it was. When they got back to their billets in the suburb of Annezin they found everything in confusion. The Welsh had been ordered to 'Stand To' in support of the 46th Division's attack:

> Our destination was the Hohenzollern Redoubt, new trench maps of which were now issued to us. The men seemed in high spirits . . . But once, when a 'mad-minute' of artillery noise began, they stopped and looked at each other. 'That's the charge,' Sergeant Townsend said sententiously. 'Many good fellows going west at this moment; maybe chums of ours.' Gradually the noise died down, and at last a message came from brigade that we would not be needed. It had been another dud show, chiefly notorious for the death of Charles Sorley, a 20-year-old captain in the Suffolks, one of the three poets of importance killed during the war. [The other two were Isaac Rosenberg and Wilfred Owen.] So ended the operations for 1915.

The *Official History* summed up the day's events in two sentences: 'The fighting had not improved the general situation in any way and had brought nothing but useless slaughter of infantry. What the British won was lost again for an insufficient supply of effective hand grenades.'

★　　★　　★

Captain Milne's photograph of the 46th Division's attack against the Hohenzollern Redoubt shows a treeless plain with a road running from left to right in the foreground. Several lines of white chalk – spoil from the British trenches – recede into the distance. The British front line, marked by the thickest width of spoil, seems to be about half a mile from where the photographer is standing. The chalk shines white in the autumn sunshine. The line of the horizon is obscured by battle haze. Black and white detonations mark where the British barrage is falling on the German positions, partly obscuring the lethal bulk of Fosse 8 slag-heap. It is impossible to tell if the black dots are men or blemishes.

I took a photograph from the same spot, crossed the same road and followed the direction of the British advance across a chequer-board of fields marked out in dead-straight lines. In one field, where maize had just been harvested, fat corn ears in the mud bore an uncanny resemblance to Mills bombs. Further on, the ground had been ploughed for winter wheat.

When I reached what I took to be the line of the old British Front, I stopped to orientate my trench map. The rows of miners' cottages, a settlement known as Cité Madagascar in 1915, was still there, front left. Further left was the site of Mad Point, occupied now by a white house with a steeply pitched roof, a useful landmark for compass bearings. There was a pyramidical slag-heap to the right of the battlefield, but it was too far right to be Fosse 8 so I turned round to check where I had come from. Since the Great War the coalfield under Loos, as defined by its slag-heaps, had undergone a wholesale transformation westwards. I counted eight major slag-heaps in the distance, including one, the Double Crassier, which had been there in 1915. Fosse 8 had vanished and Cité Madagascar had been swallowed up by the grubby settlement of Auchy-les-Mines. The miners' houses were better kept than they once were, unstained by soot, but the winding gear, the pit-head, the railway wagons and all the hardware of a working colliery had gone long since. That mass killer of British infantry, Fosse 8, had been replaced by a balding patch of green for children to play on.

After the disastrous failure of the 46th Division, frontal attacks on the Hohenzollern Redoubt were abandoned by the British in favour of subterranean methods. The site of the Redoubt was eventually occupied after being obliterated by mines. Hills reproduces a photograph of the biggest of the mine craters as they appeared in 1917, when the Leicesters found themselves back in the same area as garrison troops. Some of these craters remained. The smaller ones had been filled in with domestic garbage and covered over. Of the bigger ones, it could only be a matter of time before they too disappeared under a rubbish dump of old fridges and mattresses.

I hunkered close to the earth. I could hear the electricity sizzling in the rubberised power cables overhead. A spaniel spurted out of the undergrowth, followed by a man with a shotgun. He pretended he hadn't seen me – squatting with my outspread trench maps – and stalked past without acknowledgement. The thorn bushes planted on the Hohenzollern Redoubt provided the only covert within a square mile.

I found what I had not realised I'd been looking for – something solid. It was a brass cartridge case encrusted with chalky mud, a British cartridge case that had been ejected from a Lee Enfield rifle. Dud shells and fragments of shells still littered the arable prairie. I found a bundle of barbed wire in a beet field, rusted solid like a chunky bracelet for a giantess. I stumbled over a 'toffee apple' – a spherical mortar-bomb complete with its firing pole – and left it well alone. In the distance, where the British support lines had once been, a long plume of white smoke drifted downwind from a bonfire, like chlorine gas. The man with the shotgun fired at a rabbit or pheasant. A monoplane from Lens aero club droned overhead. The hunter fired again. I closed my eyes at the Hohenzollern Redoubt on a hazy autumn evening with gunfire in my ears, thinking about Walter and the men of 'D' Company, Fifth Leicesters; and about the Queen's uncle, Frederick Bowes-Lyon of the Black Watch, buried nearby; and about the poet, Charles Hamilton Sorley, of 'D' Company, 7th Suffolks, killed on October 13th 1915, aged 20, while attacking the two trenches known as the Hairpin. Afterwards, they found this sonnet in Sorley's kit:

> *When you see millions of the mouthless dead*
> *Across your dreams in pale battalions go,*
> *Say not soft things as other men have said,*
> *That you'll remember. For you need not so.*
> *Give them not praise. For, deaf, how should they know*
> *It is not curses heaped on each gashed head?*
> *Nor tears. Their blind eyes see not your tears flow.*
> *Nor honour. It is easy to be dead.*
> *Say only this, 'They are dead.' Then add thereto,*
> *'Yet many a better one has died before.'*
> *Then scanning all the o'ercrowded mass, should you*
> *Perceive one face that you loved heretofore,*
> *It is a spook. None wears the face you knew.*
> *Great death has made all his for evermore.*

I left the Hohenzollern Redoubt alongside the uprooted railway that used to run from Vermelles to Mad Point. When the Fosse 8 mine closed down, so did the branch line. It survived only as a grassy track between two straight-ruled thorn hedges. At

Vermelles, I turned left on to the road for Hulluch (D39) and stopped at a dour concrete cross:

'To the officers, NCOs and men of the 46th Division.'

Somebody was looking after it. Somebody trimmed the little hedge, kept the weeds down and patched the awkward corners where lumps had fallen off the concrete plinth. Somebody, some-where remembered the cost to the 46th Division of not capturing the Hohenzollern Redoubt on October 13th 1915: 180 officers and 3,500 men killed, wounded or captured, mostly within the first ten minutes of the attack.

I left for home early the next morning with a heavy heart. The names of the villages along the road had once chimed like poetry to departing Englishmen: Poperinghe, where every cellar was an *estaminet*; Brandhoek, where the ambulances lived; Vlamertinghe, with its cracked church tower; Salvation Corner, where the outward bound slipped gratefully beyond range of the German guns. The same signposts – Brielen, Lijssenthoek – that had once cheered men home now had the opposite effect, tolling the knell of my return to the day job. Within a stone's throw of the ditch on either side of the road were buried the remains of uncountable British convoys – men, mules and machinery all rendered into mulch. Yet I had been unreasonably happy in Ypres. I wanted to spend the rest of my life there, enjoying its high standard of civic hygiene, breathing deeply of its moist climate, sending my children to school among the well-behaved Euro-tots. I wondered if I might be able to wangle a gardening job with the Commonwealth War Graves Commission. Wasn't I qualified by my reverence for the soil of the Salient? According to Winston Churchill, a more sacred place did not exist for the British race.

The fields of hop-poles around Abeele passed in a motorway blur. Walter, loaded with kit, had marched the same route on his way to entrain for the Battle of Loos, but there was no time for me to stop to sniff around. I barely reached Calais in time to catch the Dover ferry.

I felt ashamed of my fellow-Britishers humping their duty-free booty back to the *Patria*; *Dulce Et Decorum Est* it most definitely was not. As soon as they got aboard, the women and children stampeded for the cafeteria. Why weren't the children at school? Where were their manners? Was too much exposure to the prose of Captain J.D. Hills turning me into a prig? Or was disillusion an inevitable after-effect of trench fever? I found my stash of British money and went to buy a newspaper to hide behind. Thank God for the *Guardian*:

LONG GOODBYE FOR THE LEGIONS LOST

by Stephen Bates

They are still finding dead soldiers on the battlefields around Ypres . . . The bodies of eight Germans came to light shortly before a remembrance service this weekend at the Menin Gate in Belgium, the huge memorial which honours nearly 55,000 troops obliterated so completely in the first three years of the war that they have no known graves. The new discoveries were notified by Guy Grewez, a local businessman who organises the Last Posts which Belgian volunteer firemen sound each evening at the gate, 22,226 so far. 'If we remember just one life each evening, think how many nights we will have to return.'

Saturday's two-minute silence, marking the precise anniversary of the armistice, was held 22 minutes late because the
Belgian contingent marching from the Catholic Cathedral
was delayed. As those already present shuffled impatiently
in the Autumn sun, there was little rancour from the largely
British and mainly elderly crowd. They knew that while the
rest of the world forgets the First World War for 364 days
of the year, Ypres remembers it every night.

More than 400,000 British and colonial troops were killed
defending the line around Ypres, and a similar number of
Germans died attacking it. The British lie in 155 cemeteries
around the border town in southern Flanders. The area, now
once more a fertile and prosperous agricultural plain, was
reduced in four years' fighting to a quagmire and the town
to rubble.

Saturday's parade at Ypres was little different from a
thousand others back in Britain. A male voice choir sang
'Abide with Me'. The old incantation 'They Shall Grow
Not Old' seemed unbearably poignant as it wafted up past
those columns of names – 'those intolerably nameless names',
as Siegfried Sassoon called them – of long-dead men. On
to the bare heads below, paper poppy petals drifted down
on the breeze from the roof of the gate. The silence was
profound . . .

Nearby, former sergeant Joe Fitzpatrick, 2nd battalion
6th Manchesters, was cheerfully receiving tributes, being
photographed, joking with a baffled Swedish television crew
and showing off his medals. Joe, doughty in flat cap, glasses
gleaming and with his hearing aid perhaps not quite on full
power . . . survived three years on the Western Front before
being captured in May 1918. 'You from the *Guardian*? I used
to work for the *Guardian* as an overseer. Did you know the

59

editor Mr Scott?' he said. 'I was wounded twice, you know, and captured. This German officer stuck his revolver in my stomach and said, you come. Well, that was the end of my war. I was lucky. So many of my friends went West. You didn't know from one day to the next.'

As night fell last night, the fire brigade's buglers were back for their evening ritual of the 'Last Post', which the town has ordained will continue in perpetuity. The men are paid an hour's overtime each night. Mr Gruwez said: 'We do not want to forget. We are ready to say the war is past, but we want to keep it alive. These men fought to liberate us. We must remember them.'

Fact or fiction? That Ypres businessman: 'Gruwez' or 'Grewez'? The British barrage at the Hohenzollern: 'very encouraging' or 'not what had been promised'? Uncle Peter says Walter was buried alive at Hill 60; he showed him the scars on his neck. But Walter was never treated in hospital for neck wounds. And when Trench 50 was blown up by a German mine on July 23rd 1915, it was not occupied by 'D' Company but by 'B' Company. Could Walter have been attached to them? Is that how he got to the Aid Post at Larch Wood Cemetery? Or was he never at that Aid Post? Was he blown up by a different mine on a different day?

An infantry company was not an inviolable unit. Platoons, sections and individuals might be detached at any time for other duties. Following 'D' Company was my best way of tracking Walter, but it wouldn't automatically lead me to him. Every man who had ever served in 'D' Company was dead. Did that mean that Walter's movements were permanently beyond the realm of verification? I had felt close to him at Packhorse Farm, and on the road from Hesdigneul to Vermelles. But the certitude I craved

60

required something actual – some trench or building or road junction, some incontrovertibly precise spot on a map. I wanted a date, a time and a grid reference.

3

THE POSTCARD

And now those waiting dreams are satisfied;
From twilight to the halls of dawn he went . . .
          Herbert Asquith, 'The Volunteer'

B lighty was an anti–climax. I rallied my spirits with book
  lore, seeking firmer historical foundations for my next
  expedition in Walter's bootsteps. Hills and Milne provided
a wealth of tactical detail, but I knew very little about how the
Leicesters' movements fitted in to the wider strategic deployment
of the British Army. To improve my comprehension of the Great
War as narrative, I turned again to the histories. I still skipped the
chapters on the Eastern Front and Caporetto, but discovered a new
interest in Bulgaria.

On September 25th 1915, as the Fifth Leicesters lit their damp
straw at Sanctuary Wood, Bulgaria began to mobilise. Neither
Hills nor Milne found space for comment, but in London the news
shook Winston Churchill to his core. If Bulgaria was joining the
Germans, Roumania and Serbia would be invaded; if Roumania

63

and Serbia were invaded, Greece would capitulate; if Greece capitulated, the Franco-British Army fighting the Turks at Gallipoli would be attacked from the north; if the Turks at Gallipoli were reinforced from the north, they would win. Winston Churchill, the man who had staked all on Gallipoli, was staring at defeat.

As the days passed, as the Allied attacks on the Western Front faltered then failed, Churchill raised a clamour for action in the Balkans. He demanded another naval attempt to force the Dardanelles, arguing that if the Royal Navy was to suddenly appear in the Sea of Marmara it might yet give the Bulgarians pause to reconsider their allegiance. Against him was a proposal to rush troops to Salonika to establish a bridgehead for direct operations against the anticipated German and Bulgarian drive south. While the mutilated survivors of Loos were being unloaded at Charing Cross railway station, the nearby corridors of the War Office resounded to the clash of Salonikans versus Gallipolites.

The Cabinet considered the arguments and couldn't agree. Under intense pressure to do something, they ordered the despatch of reinforcements in a generally eastward direction. Six British divisions would be withdrawn from France and sent to Egypt as a first expedient, their ultimate destination to be decided later. The feeling was growing among the Allies that their bit of the War was going badly wrong. Joffre's two-pronged master-stroke had been blunted with disastrous casualties; the toe-hold at Gallipoli was looking ever more precarious; the Russians were definitely weakening. For the Germans and the Central Powers, however, success was breeding success. On the Western Front they had repulsed the best that the Allies could throw at them and had retained dominance at every point; in the East they were pushing the Russian steamroller back whence it came; in the Balkans Roumania and Serbia were poised to fall.

As the first winter frosts cemented the stalemate in the West, attention fastened on the Balkans. The French came down categorically on the side of Salonika. They proposed sending an army there immediately, and asked the British to do the same. Specifically, the French wanted the British divisions marked down for Egypt to be sent straight to Salonika. Complete waste of time, said the British generals. The Serbs would be smashed in weeks, Allied troops would arrive far too late to make a difference. And anyway it was in the West, in France and Flanders, that the War would be won. Salonika and Gallipoli were side-shows dreamed up by the politicians. The French carried the day: Salonika yes, Gallipoli no.

Roumania collapsed amid the winter snows. The Serbs were crushed and dispersed. The first Franco-British troops to reach Salonika sat around and waited. They were given hardly any artillery and precious little ammunition. David Lloyd George accused the generals of trying to strangle the expedition at birth. At Gallipoli, plans were put in place for a mass evacuation. By Christmas, with the slickness of a West End transfer, the 'Tragedy of the Dardanelles' had been replaced by 'Salonika – the new Pantomime'.

Winston Churchill had already resigned. His eclipse as a statesman-strategist had left him feeling betrayed, humiliated and friendless. He quit the corridors of power for the trenches – and the possibility of a revengeful death on an ungrateful world. He had wanted a brigade command; they eventually gave him a battalion of Jock Fusiliers near Plugstreet.

The Christmas of 1915 was one of the most miserable of Churchill's life, but four miles away the Fifth Leicesters celebrated with gusto. The Line was muddy and lousy with snipers but their yule had been blessed by the glow of Eastern promise. Instead of Siberia, which is what some of the rumours had predicted for them, the 46th Division was heading for Egypt. The minarets of

Cairo beckoned. No more bully-beef, no more chloride-tainted tea. From now on each man would have a servant in a fez and a harem of concubines to feed him sherbert.

No one on that journey ever forgot it, or ceased to treasure the memory. The Fifth Leicesters entrained on January 6th 1916, in holiday mood, heading where the sun blazed, not the guns. Destination: Marseille.

The train set off at dusk from the little town of Berguette and spent the night meandering past Paris. Morning dawned crisp and blue, the men slid back the doors to let in the unseasonably warm sunshine. They lounged on the running boards or basked on the roofs of their cattle trucks. They waved at the children and hooted at the ladies. They scrambled for 'vin blong', omelettes and *frites* at every station. At Arles they saw palm trees. For the first time, they were experiencing France as a country not as a war zone. Suspended between departure and arrival, they faced no more daunting an objective than to watch the vineyards roll by. When they reached Marseille they marched into camp at Santi, a western suburb, and went straight on the spree.

The weather, according to Hills, was 'delicious'. The artillery made themselves comfortable at the racecourse, using the main stand as a barn for their fodder. Bombing practice was held at the beach. The officers lobbed grenades from the rocks while the men dived in to gather the fish that floated to the surface. Every evening, after polishing their brasswork, the Leicesters descended on the narrow streets and alleys of the Old Port to try their luck.

It has been unreliably estimated that in 1915 there were upwards of 4,000 brothels in Marseille. At Santi Camp there were compulsory lectures about sexual hygiene from the Medical Officer, and stern words about military discipline from the Provost-Sergeant. Everyone was warned to avoid the back streets at night and keep to the tram-tracks if they didn't want to come back with a black eye and empty pockets. Everyone got into debt. Nobody wanted to leave.

On January 20th 1916, orders arrived to say that the transport was ready. The next morning, the Fifth Leicesters marched down to the docks and filed up the gangplanks in platoon order. The *Aldania* was a Cunard steamer, agleam with electric chandeliers and polished mahogany. Every man had a bunk, every officer a cabin. Lunch on the first day was soup, roast beef and rice pudding. The men ate like proper toffs, off Cunard china with Cunard cutlery. 'The War,' says Milne, 'seemed to be getting better and better.'

That evening, after stowing the men below decks, the younger officers settled down for a monster game of bridge in the saloon. The air was thick with cigar smoke and brandy fumes when the Adjutant appeared – white-faced, ghastly-looking – flapping a message. Although half of the 46th Division had already left for Egypt, the remainder was being ordered to turn round. Disembarkation would proceed at 0700 hours.

Santi Camp had become hateful. The fleshpots of Marseille had ceased to allure. Visions of the Pyramids by moonlight faded. In their place stood the deathly slopes of Spanbroekmoelen, Hill 60, and Fosse 8. The blazing sands of the Arabian desert turned into Flanders mud, the sparkling Mediterranean into Zillebeke Lake. Everyone assumed the worst – The Salient again.

The Leicesters spent a grumpy week unpacking and repacking their stores. One man, Private Gregory of 'D' Company, was knocked down by a tram and killed. He was buried with full military honours. At dawn the next day, January 28th 1916, the Leicesters sent their last postcards and set their faces for the Western Front once more.

4

VIMY RIDGE

I have a rendezvous with Death
On some scarred slope of battered hill,
When Spring comes round again this year
And the first meadow-flowers appear.
        Alan Seeger, killed in action, 1916,
                    'Rendezvous'

We had been planning to take our family holiday on the west coast of Scotland, at a place between the hills and the sand dunes where, in previous years, our children – Phoebe aged seven, Gabriel aged three – had discovered a talent for living outdoors. There were rock pools and pony rides; a mysterious loch whose depths were unknown; whale-spotting trips to the islands . . .

'Vimy Ridge?'

There was no clever way to raise the subject. I just blurted it out one night. My wife loved France.

'Vimy Ridge!?'

My wife had lived in France before we married. She loved French manners and French shops, the way they dressed their children. She loved Paris and Brittany and the Pyrenees. Vimy Ridge contained that grubby bit of the Western Front where Walter had been shot.

'No way.'

I bought a tent. Later, I added sleeping-bags and a neat little gas cooker of the type I had once used as a Boy Scout. On the day of departure, Phoebe packed five Barbie dolls, Gabriel his car-transporter lorry, fully loaded. They were both grumpy because of their mother's propaganda that we ought to be heading in the opposite direction.

The nearest camp-site to Vimy Ridge was seven miles away at Béthune, a once thriving coal town which had since turned to the leisure industry for survival, replacing its redundant pits with shopping malls and converting its slag-heaps into ski slopes. The municipal camp-site had been installed on the sub-foundations of a former coal depot in the ex-industrial suburb of Beuvry. The mineralised topsoil was black with toxicity and stubbornly resistant to tent pegs. The amenities were adequate rather than *chic*: communal lavatories (without seats); wasp-infested garbage bins (emptied twice weekly); tennis rackets for hire (10 francs per person, subject to availability).

From London, it took us five hours to get to Béthune; it took the Fifth Leicesters five weeks. With half of the 46th Division in Egypt, British GHQ didn't have the slightest idea what to do with the rest. Without their artillery, the Leicesters were of little use except as raw manpower. Hills records sourly that they were set to work building railways and supply dumps in preparation for the Big Push of 1916:

We were always living on the verge of the Big Push, and many times in 1915 had thought that it had started – at Neuve Chapelle, Givenchy, Loos – only to give up hope when these battles had stagnated after a day or two. Now there were preparations going forward again, this time on a much larger scale than we had ever seen before . . .

The Germans had plans for a Big Push of their own. On February 21st 1916, they hurled themselves at the southern French fortress of Verdun with unheralded ferocity. Sir Douglas Haig, now promoted to British Commander-in-Chief, had already agreed to relieve some French troops, but the blitzkrieg at Verdun forced Joffre to ask the British to take on an extra 20 miles of the Western Front at once. In describing the new terrain – running from Loos south to the River Somme – the British Official Historian, James Edmonds, forswore his customary drab for an experiment in colour:

> After the dreary and depressing surroundings of Flanders, the new area, dry and bright, with No Man's Land a wide stretch of scarlet poppies, yellow mustard, red clover and blue cornflowers, was a pleasant contrast. The spirits of the troops rose accordingly, the ground seemed made for a successful battle.

It was not a 'pleasant contrast' as far as the Leicesters were concerned. While the Kitchener volunteers and Regulars were given dry trenches with a botanically enhanced view of No Man's Land, the Terriers of the 46th Division were sent to the corpse-ridden battlefield of Vimy Ridge. In footballing terms it was a depressing away fixture – yet another uphill slog against a notoriously difficult defence. As at Hill 60 and Spanbroekmoelen, the Fifth Leicesters found themselves clinging to a bleak slope of grey mud while the Germans looked down with arrogant impunity.

Vimy's trenches were in a shocking state. As Milne explains:

They were dirty because they had been occupied by dirty troops. For the French Army standard of cleanliness is not the same as ours. A dead animal or two in the vicinity does not worry them. And any old place is good enough for any old latrine. The French are great fighters, great thinkers, great artists. But collectively, their proclivity for tidiness is not pronounced, and their sense of smell is undoubtedly deficient.

On paper, the French defences consisted of three lines of trenches. These proved to be illusory. The French had relied for defence on the efficiency of their quick-firing field guns, the 75s. In some places their front line was marked by just a few sandbags thrown on the ground. 'With the French,' says Hills, 'there is no doubt that [the Germans] had a tacit understanding not to wage a vigorous war, though, while seeming inactive, they had all the while been undermining the French trenches.'

The Fifth Leicesters took over from the French 68th Regiment on the evening of March 9th 1916. The next day was quiet. The Germans tried a few pot-shots and threw a single grenade. The Leicesters replied with two. The following morning, March 11th, the Germans probed a little harder and threw six grenades. The Leicesters replied with ten. This, according to Hills, convinced the Germans that their little local truce was over:

At 4.45 p.m. they blew up a small mine opposite A Company, demolished a sap-head, and half-buried the solitary occupant, who escaped with bruises. After this, they bombed, or tried to bomb us, until 8.00 p.m., while we replied at the rate of two-to-one.

The routine of the Fifth Leicesters at Vimy Ridge was as follows: six days in the front line; six days in support; six days in reserve; six days' rest. The front line lay about two-thirds of the way up the ridge. The support positions lay at the bottom, in Zouave Valley. Where the hillside was steepest was called Talus des Zouaves – an embankment honeycombed with solid, deep dugouts which had been dug by the Germans before their withdrawal to the top of the hill. Although the Germans knew the terrain well, the steepness of the Talus made it immune to their artillery, except for 'sausages' – the mortar bombs that were among their deadliest trench weapons. 'The battalion in support lived in some comfort,' says Milne, 'but outside the atmosphere was charged with the sizzle of sausages and the stench of Zouaves.'

The Zouaves, French colonial troops from North Africa, had tried to take Vimy Ridge at the same time as the British first tried to take the Hohenzollern Redoubt, with similar results: they'd swarmed up the hill and seized the German line temporarily before being bundled back to their start positions. 'They lost terribly,' says Milne, 'and their dead lay just as they fell in their red coats and white trousers, which the winter had now turned nearly as black as their faces.'

The Leicesters spent their time at the Talus humping stores, tinkering with home-made bombs (launched by catapult) and deepening trenches. Rations and ammunition were dragged up by mules on a narrow-gauge railway. The danger in the front line came from mining – which was being pursued energetically by both sides – and sniping. A favourite German tactic was to mortar-bomb the British trenches and then snipe the men brought forward for rebuilding work. On the chalky soil of Vimy Ridge it only needed a momentary silhouette, day or night, for a marksman to score.

Goatskin coats were issued to keep out the cold; steel helmets made their first appearance to ward off shrapnel. Thigh-length waders would have been useful. Alternate frosts and thaws filled the trenches with mud, undermining all efforts at improvement. Parapets and parados collapsed wholesale. As Hills writes:

Our stay in a warm climate had made us less capable of standing exposure to cold and wet, and there were many cases of trench fever, trench foot and some pneumonia. One of the most pitiful sights of the War was to see 20 of our men crawling on hands and knees to the Aid Post – their feet so bad that they could not walk.

It was here, to the Aid Post in the Talus des Zouaves, that Walter crawled or hobbled after he was shot. His medical card in the Public Record Office at Kew – the one that had told me his Company – says he was admitted to No. 6 General Hospital on April 19th 1915: 'G.S.W. foot Lt. Received four days ago. Condition slight. Well on discharge.'

If the wound had been 'received four days ago', Walter must have been hit on April 15th 1915. Hills makes no specific reference to this day's events, so before leaving England I had gone to check his original source, the Fifth Leicesters' *War Diary*.

Every British infantry battalion on active service kept a *War Diary*, the maintenance of which fell to the Adjutant. As the number of experienced Adjutants fell rapidly, through wastage or promotion, the administrative chores of infantry battalions came to be delegated to increasingly junior officers. The job paid 25 shillings a day and carried the acting rank of Captain, but it was a thankless grind and those who did it got no rest. They were expected to do their full whack as Company officers in trenches and catch up with the office work when they came out. More than a dozen different signatures authenticated the loose foolscap forms of the Fifth Leicesters' *War Diary* at Kew:

14.4.16. Battalion moved from huts (Camblain L'Abbé) to trenches and relieves 4th Lincs. Relief completed 10.30 pm. Dispositions –   A Coy. Reserve.

B Coy. Right sector; 2 platoons front line, 2 support.

C Coy. Boissillet Support.

D Coy. Left sector; 2 platoons front line, 2 support.

Previous to our taking over, enemy had exploded a mine on left sector and had blown in one of our sap heads. Although enemy's fire had subsided somewhat at time of relief a lot of work had to be done in building up parapet and cleaning trench.

15.4.16. Shelled badly during afternoon, part of front line parapet being blown in on left sector. Right sector quiet.

8 pm–4 am, A Coy provided two working parties, 8–12 12–4, digging new support line.

8 pm–4 am, C Coy carried rations for Coys in front line, also provided digging party to repair Boissillet Tr.

Casualties – 2 NCO's, 2 men.

Cross-reference to the medical records at Kew (MH 1062131/8675) confirmed that '1 NCO' and '2 men' of the Fifth Leicesters were admitted to hospital on April 19th 1915. (The one unaccounted-for NCO was presumably so lightly wounded that he didn't require hospital treatment, or so badly wounded that he died before getting there.) The '1 NCO' who had been hit, Lance-Corporal Ferrin of 'C' Company, was admitted to No. 6 General Hospital with a 'G.S.W. arm R.' Luckily, it was a severe wound and after four days at Rouen he was transferred to England. The '2 men' who had been injured missed out on a Blighty and had to stay in France. One of them was Walter, with his 'G.S.W. foot Lt.' The other was a fellow Private in 'D' Company called Stevens, who was admitted with a 'G.S.W. leg R.' It seemed likely – since both men were from the same Company and were admitted to hospital on the same day with similar wounds – that they had been hit in the same incident, if not by the same volley of shots. The fact that they were both hit low down suggested that they weren't in a trench at the time. They must have been caught out on top, taking part in some 'vigorous retaliation' perhaps, or repairing the left sector parapet which had been blown in by German shellfire. If Privates Butterworth and Stevens had been doing anything gallant when they were hit, they might have won a more detailed mention in the *War Diary*, although probably not. Whereas every officer who served with the Fifth Leicesters, no matter how junior or for how short a time, was scrupulously identified, NCOs and men were not. Officers came individually or in pairs; they had names. Men came in drafts of dozens or scores; they were anonymous.

As soon as the Fifth Leicesters volunteered for overseas service, Walter Butterworth had ceased to exist as an individual personality. As far as the British Army was concerned, he had surrendered his identity for the duration of the War; he had become a unit of military manpower – '1 man'.

'Take that man's name, Corporal, his shirt's hanging out.'

'Send a section of men out when it's dark, Captain Shields, and put that parapet back.'

Only to himself and his comrades in 'D' Company did Walter remain unique. To his officers he was human materiel, useful or not according to purpose. He was rescued from this oblivion not by his courage but by his vulnerability. Walter could have done the bravest deed in the world on Vimy Ridge on April 15th 1916, and still he might have died unknown. The reward for gallantry depended on a reliable officer surviving to report it. In getting wounded, however, Walter became grist to the vast bureaucratic mill that sustained the British Army in the field. His personal documents – pay-book, letters, discharge papers – were his to lose or discard after the War, which is why they had all been lost or discarded. The documentation listing Walter's career as a casualty belonged to the Army, which is how his 'G.S.W. foot Lt.' came to be preserved for posterity.

I began my search for Walter's trench at the village of Souchez, at the north end of Zouave Valley. Most of the inhabitants had fled. The *café-tabac* was open, and the *boulangerie*, but the rest of the village was blind for the August holiday, shuttered tight against a downpour of yellow sunshine. The traffic consisted of a postman on his velo and a lonely dog. An old lady fussed with her window-box. Was she old enough, I wondered, to know Souchez?

The French writer, Henri Barbusse, knew Souchez. He served at Vimy Ridge and describes in his masterpiece *Under Fire* how he was taken to Souchez during a lull in the battle by a comrade who had once lived there:

> It is a flat field, carpeted with broken bricks. And what is that there? A milestone? No, it is not a milestone. It is a head, a black head, tanned and polished. The mouth is all askew, and you can see something of the moustache bristling on each side – the great head of a carbonised cat. The corpse – it is German – is underneath, buried upright [. . .] My companion

says nothing, but looks to right and to left. Then he stops
again, as he did at the top of the road. I hear his faltering
voice, almost inaudible – 'What's this! We're there – this
is it—' In point of fact we have not left the plain, the vast
plain, seared and barren – but we are in Souchez! The village
has disappeared, nor have I seen a village go so completely
[. . .] There is not even an end of wall, fence, or porch that
remains standing; and it amazes one to discover that there
are paving-stones under the tangle of beams, stones and scrap
iron. This – here – was a street.

A sign erected by the Commonwealth War Graves Commission
directed me out of the village on to a part-metalled farm track liberally
spattered with cowpats and tractor mud. Behind the hedgerows, busy
with dragonflies, Zouave Valley whispered its welcome. I knew from
Barbusse what was hidden to right and to left:

The Zouaves had all begun to dig themselves individual
shelters, and round these they were exterminated. Some
are still seen, prone on the brim of an incipient hole with
their trenching tools in their fleshless hands or looking at
them with the cavernous hollows where shrivel the entrails
of eyes. The ground is so full of dead that the earth-falls
uncover places bristling with feet, with half-clothed skeletons,
and with ossuaries of skulls placed side by side on the steep
slope like porcelain globe jars . . .

I passed through the shadow of the valley of death and stopped
to orientate myself at Zouave Valley Cemetery, a useful fixed
point occupying the angle between two tracks marked clearly
on my trench map. On April 15th 1915, the Fifth Leicesters had
been holding the left of this sector, between Ersatz Trench and

International Trench. These two communication trenches were clearly marked on my map, so I climbed through the fence and began my ascent.

The sunken course of the communication trench known as Uhlan Alley was still visible as a set of sunken traverses in the grass, but Ersatz Trench and International Trench ('a catastrophe of flesh and filthiness' when Barbusse slithered up it) had disappeared. My tracks must have intersected with Walter's more than a dozen times as I zigzagged up the side of Vimy Ridge, but I knew from the start that I wasn't going to find what I was looking for. A monster had come along and scarred Zouave Valley more permanently than any wound inflicted by the Great War. The old British front line had been replaced by a motorway, the A26–E15 autoroute from Calais to Paris, gouging across the slope of Vimy Ridge like a sabre slash.

I held to the fence by the side of the motorway and watched the traffic speeding by. The immense land mass known as Europe shuddered beneath the soles of my boots every time a heavy lorry rumbled past. Had I been minded, I could have walked to Berlin or Moscow or Vladivostock. I could not have walked to Hinckley. Europe was not part of me, nor any part of the way I looked at the world. The surrounding particularities of place – grass, leaves, traffic fumes – could have been anywhere in England, except for their being bleached of all vital familiarity.

Around Ypres I had felt almost at home in the landscape; on Vimy Ridge I felt diminished. The thought that I might ever have been able to find Walter's old trench seemed stupid to me, now that I could see what had happened to it. 'Get real,' urged the drivers on the motorway, 'look to the future, forget the past. Bond with the idea of Europe as an ever-expanding family of Euro-states with Germany at its head.'

A torn page of an illustrated magazine fluttered on the wire, less like a clue than a scrap of info-carrion. I deciphered something in a foreign language about a lottery, and something else about a TV celebrity's new boyfriend. To an Englishman it was meaningless, like a practical joke without point or pay-off. Maybe I deserved a face full of diesel fumes for being the insular, backward-looking trench hog that I was. Walter was shot at Vimy Ridge for the sake of Europe, but when the job was over he was glad never to see the place again.

Zouave Valley Cemetery was small and square, unrelieved by any rhetorical flourish. It contained only one Leicester, a 'Known unto God'. The rest were mainly Londoners. Walter would not have recognised the place. In his day, the British dead were taken further back for burial, on the empty mule-trains which had brought up the rations. Zouave Valley Cemetery was not begun until May 1916, by which stage the Fifth Leicesters had left the Talus for ever.

The pages of the Visitors' Book at the cemetery showed an average summer attendance of a dozen British pilgrims per month. Trevor Bishop of Wigan had written: 'Tranquillity epitomised.' K. Handforth from Huddersfield had written: 'Peaceful setting. R.I.P.' What they had meant to write, surely, was: 'Bloody motorway!' Or: 'Shame about the noise.' Mr and Mrs Winterton from Hatfield Peverel still wanted to believe in the *entente cordiale*: 'Nice to see the cemetery is visited by French children from Souchez.' Perhaps they were being ironic. The written contributions of the children of Souchez – 'France 2 – 1 Allemagne'; 'FUCK ME'; '*Je vois des cul partout*' – suggested that whatever the purpose of their visit, it had not been for melancholic retrospection.

Sixty thousand Canadians died on the Western Front during the Great War. Their bereaved compatriots were given a slice of it afterwards, as a token of gratitude. At the highest point of Vimy Ridge, on land ceded to the people of Canada in perpetuity, they built a monument dedicated to all those who'd fallen, but especially to the 11,285 Canadians whose bodies were never found: The Missing. The monument consists of two massive pylons – Canada and France – draped with symbolic sculptures. The pylons spring from a common base and taper towards each other, defining an upward space so eloquent of something missing. When I switched my attention down to the symbolic resting-place of Canada's lost sons, I experienced a jolt of vertigo. The monument's white Dalmatian stone was cool to the touch, but it reflected sunlight so harshly that it brought tears to my eyes.

The Canadians who built the memorial at Vimy Ridge had thought it was a fine and fitting thing to die for one's country, even if that country was part of someone else's Empire. The same memorial today reminds modern visitors that war in general is a waste, and that the Great War was especially futile. When construction began, Vimy Ridge was still in a state of despoliation. Scavengers gleaned for copper and brass among the dud shells that littered the site. Today, it is one of the few places on the Western Front where the opposing trench systems can still be seen, although the original sandbags and duckboards have been replaced by concrete ones to maintain the shape of the trenches and prevent them being worn away by visitors' footsteps. To understand the scale of the Canadians' triumph, it is only necessary to stand in their old trenches and imagine the fissured hillside above them swarming with Germans pouring down unremitting fire. In places, the German positions were only ten yards away from the Canadian front line. At 0530 hours, April 9th 1917, the Canadians climbed out of these trenches, ducked their heads against the storm of steel and lunged forward.

Step by step, objective by objective, they worked their way

up the slope, hugging the ground for cover, fighting shoulder to shoulder for the honour of their country. It was the first time the Canadians had gone into battle as a national contingent. They were delayed briefly at Hill 145, the place where the foundations of the Vimy monument would one day rest, but by afternoon the Germans had been swept from the heights and were retreating towards Lens. To follow the line of the Canadians' advance from their trenches to their monument is to make both a symbolic and a literal ascent: from darkness to light; from fear to courage; from defeat to victory.

The vast numbers of French, British and German soldiers who perished on or around Vimy Ridge made its name notorious throughout the world. The close proximity of so many war cemeteries makes it a study of the differing national attitudes to The Fallen. The French may be great fighters, great thinkers and great artists, but their restraint in funerary matters is not pronounced. Their memorial at Notre Dame de Lorette, above Souchez, revels in unexpected vulgarity. The 19,000 individual concrete crosses have not grown old gracefully. The burial plots are separated by harsh red gravel and thorny beds of roses. The cumulative effect is one of regimented bleakness, and there is something incongruous about the unabashedly phallic, neo-Byzantine lighthouse chosen to dominate the cemetery and its chapel of remembrance. An inscription declares that the intention was to guard the memory of The Fallen against the remorseless oblivion of Night. But what symbolic associations connect lighthouses to the brave foot-soldiers of the Republic? The nearest beach to Souchez is 80 miles away.

No flags fly over the glorious dead at Zouave Valley Cemetery, nor the score of British cemeteries around Vimy Ridge. Each one contains the same cross and the same stone. The cross stands for sacrifice; the stone for remembrance. There is no striving for emotional effect, just a line of scripture: 'Their name liveth for evermore.'

British war cemeteries were conceived not as Golgothas but as Gethsemanes. Their architecture eschewed drama for the quieter virtues of the English country garden – low stone walls, flagstone paths, green lawns. Perhaps a terrace or an arcade of Doric columns. Sculptural decoration was restricted to the spare use of the basic motifs of imperial tradition – lions' heads, oak leaves, laurel.

Each dead soldier of the British Empire was worth the same. The son of the Prime Minister was given the same headstone as the son of the Prime Minister's blacksmith. It was 32 inches high and 15 inches across. It bore the name of the interred and his rank, his age, date of death and his military decorations. If the dead soldier's regiment was known, his headstone was carved with the regimental badge. If nothing was known, the headstone said simply, 'A soldier of the Great War – Known unto God.' Relatives were allowed to add an inscription at the bottom, providing it did not consist of more than 60 characters.

Many of the British dead attained a dignity in death that was denied them in life. Their self-sacrifice was deemed to have invalidated all previous disqualifications of cult or caste. Sinner or saint, Great Death embraced them all. Visiting the graves of this democratic brotherhood can be addictive to those of a nostalgic disposition. Particularities of locale – clay or chalk, field or hill – infuse each cemetery with a sense of personality. The serried headstones of a British cemetery reveal the mongrel diversity of many races in one nation: Lincolns and Leicesters; Connaughts and Cameronians; Suffolks and Surreys. The brilliant and the brave, as John Buchan wrote, all part of that immortal country which knows not age nor weariness nor defeat.

When the French cleared their battlefields, the collected piles of mismatched skulls and bones were dumped in mass graves and ossuaries. Notre Dame de Lorrette has six such pits, containing the remains of 16,000 men. It was a compact and cheap solution, but it was repugnant to British sentiment. For the purposes of winning the Great War, men's individuality was disposable; in death it became sacrosanct. Every British cemetery became a temple to the uniqueness of each of The Fallen.

In their different ways, British and French cemetery-makers sought to express honour, gratitude and love for their dead sons. When the Germans retreated, their dead had to fend for themselves. A single brass button with a regimental crest was enough to give an unknown British soldier a semblance of identity when the great gathering-in took place. Nothing served to distinguish dead Germans from one another. When the tide of war flowed East at last, those Germans left behind were jetsam.

Travelling south from Vimy Ridge, I found the main German cemetery – Neuville St Vaast – on the site of a trench-work once known as The Labyrinth, a German position of evil renown that withstood repeated attacks throughout the first two years of the War. The Labyrinth was a maze of trenches protected by thick barbed wire and ingeniously sited machine guns; it claimed thousands of victims before its defenders were driven out. By then its chalk craters were a clotted shambles of human remains and shredded uniforms. J.B. Priestley (No. 8 Platoon, 'B' Company, 10th Duke of Wellington's, 69th Brigade, 23rd Division) was among the first English troops into the Labyrinth after its trenches were taken over from the French: '. . . when we explored them we found them filled with bloodstained clothing, abandoned equipment, heads, legs and arms.'

King George's soldiers, sleeping their final sleep in Zouave Valley Cemetery, had fought the good fight and their names would live for evermore; there were no fine words for the Kaiser's men at Neuville St Vaast. These 45,000 Germans lie where they were hated, in mass graves. The cemetery's fixtures and fittings emphasise the finality of death: black crosses; flat slabs; lumpen sculpture. There were trees, but no flowers, for who would have tended them? The French and British had died for a reason: to defend their homes against Germans. The Germans had died . . . for what? They had been duped. Defeat had lost them their rights to remembrance.

I walked through Neuville St Vaast Cemetery, down aisles of black crosses, trying to pronounce the unfamiliar German names: Fritz Endalein, *soldat*; Michael Hyszak, *musketier*; Arthur Reier, *soldat*; Ernst Oelker, *gefreiter*; Stanislaus Matuszewski, *jager*. Name after name, row after row, acre after acre, all unbearably meaningless. The markers were laid out with such precision that, as I passed between them, the rows of crosses narrowed magically into parallax lines and disappeared. Who were they? The dead. Why had they come? To die.

During the War, the Germans had earned a reputation for having the best graveyards of any of the combatants, with stone grave-markers and elaborate carvings for men as well as for officers. Occasionally they would honour the graves of their enemies in like manner, something the British and the French never did. Yet there were no honoured or tranquil graves at Neuville St Vaast; it was bleak with shame and full of forgetfulness.

Death. Death was everywhere. It was at the camp-site, in the supermarket, in every leaf, beyond the horizon. So much Death had been concentrated into the fields around Vimy Ridge and Béthune and Beuvry that it posed a direct personal challenge. Was mortality behind my Great War obsession – the idea that within the ranks of the numberless dead I might recognise my own extinction? Was this what I was looking for in my search for Walter, a space in the Great War wherein I might have served?

Vimy Ridge had cheated me of Walter's trench, but there were other possibilities. The Béthune–Lens sector contained several localities associated with the Fifth Leicesters in the later stages of the War; they'd spent the Christmas of 1917 in Beuvry and had stayed until the following spring. Remaining to explore these associations would have been the sensible thing to do, but by this stage I was in the acute phase of full-blown trench fever. From Vimy Ridge, Walter's trail led straight to the Battle of the Somme, and the bloodiest place on the bloodiest day of British military history – to Gommecourt, July 1st 1916.

5

GOMMECOURT

. . . and instantly the whole sky burned
With fury against them; and soft sudden cups
Opened in thousands for their blood; and the green slopes
Chasmed and steepened sheer to infinite space.

Wilfred Owen, killed in action, 1918,
'Spring Offensive'

Walter was convalescing after treatment for his 'G.S.W. foot Lt.' when the Fifth Leicesters were withdrawn from Vimy to be sent south. He rejoined them in one of the 'large drafts' that Hills reports arriving during the first weeks of May. By this stage the battalion was billeted at Lucheux, a village ten miles from the Front which derived its vaguely Cotswold atmosphere from a ruined castle and a stream of pure water gurgling down the valley. Each morning the officers would exercise the regimental horses in the grounds of the château while the men were led into the ancient forest to make wattle revetments for the distant trenches. 'It was a delightful way of spending the merry month of May,' says Milne. 'The wood was shady. The birds sang in the trees. Contented soldiers whistled through their teeth.'

The 46th Division was being fattened for the Big Push. New kit was issued, back pay was brought up to date, the food was improved in quality and quantity. As the hedgerows blossomed and the green shoots grew thicker in the cornfields, the Leicesters felt themselves reviving:

> Life could be very happy if one only looked twenty-four hours ahead [says Milne]. The girl at the *estaminet* who sold the flamboyant postcards seemed quite friendly and had nice eyes; rather like those of the calf that has just been born at the farm. The tits made a lot of noise in the early morning over plans for nest building. And there was a rooster who got up so early and made such a noise that it was a wonder the hens did not mutiny.

As the sap rose all over Picardy, Hills stayed conspicuously immune. He notes that the billets were 'good', that the weather was 'fine' and that the work on revetments was 'not too hard'. Mostly, though, he finds Lucheux interesting for the new emphasis it brought to the Fifth Leicesters' training programme: 'For many months now we had been taught the bomb to the exclusion of almost every other weapon, now at last the bayonet was returning to its former position of importance.'

The Leicesters were visited by Major Ronnie Campbell V.C., of the Army Gymnastic Staff. The War, he declared, was not going to be won by sitting in trenches. As the occupying force, the Germans could afford to dig in and sit tight; the Allies could not. Their job was to attack the invader and drive him back. And the spirit of the attack was the spirit of the bayonet. Major Campbell did away with the textbook 'points' and 'parries' of pre-1914 bayonet drill and substituted a simpler scheme based on stabbing. Two inches was enough for the throat, four inches for the kidneys. 'For two hours,' says Hills, 'he held the attention of a hall half-full of all ranks, speaking so vividly that not one of us but came away feeling that we were good enough to fight six Boche, given a bayonet.'

The brushing-up of bayonet handling wasn't the only clue. Kitchener battalions were pouring into the Somme in unprecedented numbers. The air at Lucheux thickened with rumour and premonition. On May 20th 1916, the Fifth Leicesters kissed goodbye to the girls with nice eyes, to say nothing of the cocks and tits. They marched east to the village of Souastre, where they spent the next month plumbing in the infrastructure for the imminent offensive – pipelines, railways, roads, trenches, gun-pits, supply dumps. Hills detected an ominous turn in the weather: 'One day it was so hot as to make continuous work for more than a few hours impossible. The next day, there would be three or four torrential rain storms, filling all the trenches and turning the cross-country tracks to avenues of mud.'

We left Beuvry for Souastre under a cloudless sky. My wife was in the driving seat so that I could concentrate on the landscape and its Great War associations. There wasn't a name on the map that didn't evoke a sense of recognition. Each town, each village, each bridge and crossroads was part of English folklore. It felt profligate to be whooshing past it all – Vermelles, Bully-Grenay, Lens – at motorway speed.

'Look, Phoebe, there's the monument we went to.'

A gap opened in the pine trees and there for an instant, angel-white against postcard-blue, shone Vimy's Canadian Memorial.

'Where?'

'There!'

Gone . . . It was all too remote. Where I saw battlefields and the clash of mighty themes, Phoebe saw trees and fields. We turned off the autoroute and left the lopped-off slag-heaps for the wooded downland of the Somme, the Santerre, Sancta Terra, the Sacred Land. Charlemagne had dwelt in Picardy. My head swelled with thoughts of Death and Glory.

> '"If I should die, think only this of me:
> That there's some corner of a foreign field
> That is for ever England. There shall be
> In that rich earth, a richer dust concealed . . ."'

'What's that fountain thing?' asked Phoebe.

It was an irrigator in a potato field. Phoebe was far too young for Rupert Brooke and the Battle of the Somme. So was I. The Somme was a lifetime's study, a mythology I could never hope to master.

The British Army marshalled by Sir Douglas Haig at the Somme was about ten times that of Wellington at Waterloo. The British Expeditionary Force of August 1914 had expanded from four divisions to 58 divisions by July 1916. To sustain such numbers in the field required a commensurate expansion of support units – everything from camouflage studios and veterinary hospitals to typewriter workshops. The Army even had its own rubber-stamp unit. Such specialisation, multiplied by scale, created unprecedented problems of administration.

Unfortunately for the British generals, the exponential growth of firepower in the 101 years since Waterloo had not been matched by commensurate improvements in command and control. Wellington commanded personally, in the field, on horseback. Sir Douglas Haig was not only many miles distant from the field but his subordinate commanders, once battle had commenced, were entirely cut off from reliable information about its progress and therefore unable to influence it. The artillery barrage of 1916 was so intense that every form of communication was liable to failure. Telegraph and telephone cables had to be laid six feet deep to stand even a chance of surviving. Radio was still in its infancy. Once the preliminary artillery barrage had lifted and the infantry went over the top, British commanders were enveloped in ignorance. It could take as long as six hours for an order to pass from an Army HQ to a front-line battalion in action.

To compensate for this weakness of battlefield communications, the British Staff set out to make the Big Push of 1916 a model of planning and preparation. The original Expeditionary Force had been sent into the Battle of the Marne in 1914 with orders running to six paragraphs. The orders issued by British GHQ in advance of the Somme – 'Preparatory Measures To Be Taken In Armies And Corps Before Undertaking Offensive Operations On A Large Scale' – ran to 57 pages, excluding appendices. Divisional and Brigade Commanders were instructed in every detail, from the positioning of latrines to the collection of salvage. Every contingency was to be anticipated, nothing left to chance. The typewriter inspectors and rubber-stamp makers of the British Army worked overtime as paperwork swirled between Army and Corps Headquarters. Planning proliferated at every echelon for a single compelling reason: the generals didn't trust their men.

The pre-War regular Army had ceased to exist by the summer of 1916, except as a leavening of hardy survivors in individual units. In place of the Regulars stood Kitchener's New Armies and the Territorials. The officers of the Kitchener divisions were bright and keen, their men were physically strong and highly motivated. But the vast majority had no experience of fighting. Sceptical Army and Corps Commanders regarded them as enthusiastic amateurs. Even those battalions which had gone through the trenches could hardly be described as battle-hardened, not by comparison with their enemies. One of the German army's strongest weapons was the belief that it was the best led, best trained, best equipped military force ever assembled in a European theatre. And in the summer of 1916 it was at the apogee of its power. The British generals decided there was only one way for their raw troops to make a show of it against such opposition: they would have to learn their parts by rote and stick to them. The British infantry would be drilled, drilled and drilled again until every last man knew every last detail of what he was expected to do at Zero hour. The Big Push would proceed like clockwork. Brainpower, translated into planning and training, would compensate for the troops' military deficiencies. Planning, training and preparation would win the Battle of the Somme before a shot had been fired.

To some English people, the Somme feels like home. William and Jess succumbed so completely that they swapped their bungalow in Darlington for a kit-built chalet overlooking No Man's Land. With William's early retirement package to see them through the lean months, they had launched into the bed-and-breakfast business. A defiant little Union Jack fluttered from the signboard as we pulled into the driveway: 'Billy's Billet. Gites de France.'

'See where that fence-post is, at the corner of the field? That's where the old British front line took a swerve. See over there, behind those thorn bushes? That's where the big mine went off on July the first . . .'

We couldn't afford this dugout. The cost of the tent, the sleeping-bags, the travel insurance and the cross-Channel ferry had used up more than half our permitted overdraft. On top of that we had taken the expensive precaution of having the car serviced before departure. Plus, we had joined an international breakdown recovery scheme, just in case. There was no leeway in the budget for a chalet. Unfortunately, the nearest camp-site to Gommecourt was 17 miles away.

'Malins must have been round here a lot,' mused William.

Malins . . . of course. The man who filmed the Somme. It is Geoffrey Malins' grainy footage of the action, endlessly recycled in television documentaries, that we all 'remember' as the Battle of the Somme – the stretcher-cases having their cigarettes lit, reinforcements doggedly filing up communication trenches, battle-shocked prisoners heading for the cages. This hadn't been enough for William. He had wanted the *actualité,* some corner of a foreign field to call his own.

The officers of the Fifth Leicesters were briefed about the coming fight at 46th Division HQ at Lucheux. The French, facing losses of 100,000 men a month at Verdun, were desperate for British help in the form of a strategic diversion. Accordingly, it had been decided that the British Fourth Army would attack along a 14-mile front north of the River Somme, while the French Sixth Army attacked on a 6-mile front south of the river. The British effort would be preceded by a five-day artillery bombardment designed to reach a crescendo of destructiveness in the final hour before Zero. The infantry would advance in regularly spaced waves and occupy the shattered German defences according to a timetable. Support waves would consolidate and prepare for the next jump ahead. The 46th Division had been assigned the left-most flank of the attack. Its specific objective, in a combined operation with the 56th Division, was Gommecourt, a fortified village which formed a salient in the British line.

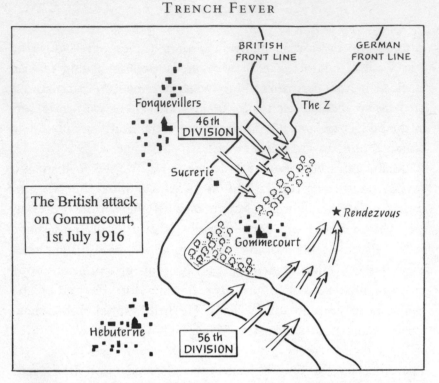

BRITISH
FRONT LINE

GERMAN
FRONT LINE

Fonquevillers

The Z

46th
DIVISION

Sucrerie

★ Rendezvous

The British attack
on Gommecourt,
1st July 1916

Gommecourt

Hebuterne

56th
DIVISION

While the main thrust of the Somme attack had been entrusted
to the Fourth Army, the 46th and 56th Divisions belonged at
this stage to the Third Army. Few in the ranks knew or cared
about such higher military abstractions as Armies or Corps, but
to generals with careers at stake such distinctions were of jealous
concern. The fact that, Gommecourt aside, the Third Army had
not been assigned any role in the biggest battle in history was not
the surest guarantee of enthusiasm from its commanders. As far as
they were concerned, the Battle of the Somme was not their show.
The purpose of their attack on Gommecourt was to draw German
reserves away from the south. There would be casualties but no
glory. If the Fourth Army broke through as expected, few laurels
would be awarded to the diversionary troops on the flank – which
is presumably why the Third Army gave the job to its Territorials.

The good news, as far as Walter was concerned, was that the

Fifth Leicesters would not be in the attack. The 138th Brigade (Lincs and Leics), would be held in reserve at Zero, in recognition of the fact that it had suffered most heavily in the 46th Division's catastrophe at the Hohenzollern Redoubt. The assault this time would be carried by the 137th Brigade (North and South Staffords) and the 139th Brigade (Sherwood Foresters). At Zero hour, the Staffords and Sherwoods would advance side by side against Gommecourt from trenches in front of the village of Fonquevillers. Simultaneously, two brigades of the 56th Division would drive into the German lines from the south, jumping off from positions in front of the village of Hebuterne. After completing this pincer movement, the attacking formations would isolate the German garrison and hammer it into surrender.

The Staffords and Sherwood Foresters practised their assault under the eyes of Divisional Staff at Lucheux, where a replica of the German trench system had been dug to a depth of two feet. To begin with, they practised moving in formation. Later, they practised with a variety of kit designed to simulate the actual loads – ladders, bombs, ammunition, baskets of pigeons – that they would have to carry into action. The assault course stretched across several fields and although Hills says the local farmers were well paid for the disruption, the 46th Division was known among them henceforth as 'les autres Boches'. As soon as the model trenches had been dug, a German plane flew over to take photographs.

While the Staffords and Sherwood Foresters drilled and re-drilled, the Fifth Leicesters held the front line at Fonquevillers. They moved into trenches opposite Gommecourt Park on June 4th. The park was said to contain the 'Kaiser's Oak', an apocryphal tree marking the furthest extent of the German advance on the Western Front. The thick woodland had been interwoven by dense belts of barbed wire, presenting a formidable obstacle. That, and the fact that the park was an appendage of no strategic value, was the reason why it had been decided to leave it alone at Zero.

The Leicesters patrolled by night. Squads with blackened faces crawled out under the wire, but didn't make contact with the Germans. Frustrated, the Leicesters set up a board in front of the German wire with what Hills calls an 'insulting message' on it. The back of the notice had been marked with luminous paint and a machine gun was trained on it, should the Germans be provoked into taking the bait. They were not. They had no need to reconnoitre because they knew what was coming. Quite apart from what German air reconnaisance had seen at Lucheux, the British had been ordered to advertise their offensive intentions by digging new jumping-off trenches in No Man's Land. It was all part of the business of luring German units away from other parts of the Line. 'It became exceedingly dangerous,' says Hills, 'for the Boche, knowing exactly where we were working, swept the ground continuously with accurate machine-gun fire.'

The British artillery behind Fonquevillers started registering their guns on June 24th. The batteries of the 46th Division were allotted 400 rounds per gun per day to cut lanes through the German wire and pulverise selected strongpoints in the Gommecourt defences. As Zero hour approached, the bombardment intensified to 700 rounds per gun per day. Hills says the German guns replied by registering British communications and then stayed silent.

Hills' interest in the artillery preparations was caused by a late change in divisional orders. After practising their attack several times, the Staffords had discovered that they had 'more tasks to fulfil than they could accomplish' and had asked 138th Brigade for the loan of an extra battalion. The Fifth Leicesters were offered because they had suffered least at the Hohenzollern. Three companies of Fifth Leicesters were ordered to form an

extra line behind the Staffords' attack. They would hump stores
and ammunition across No Man's Land to keep up the momentum
of the advance once the German defences had been breached.
The fourth company would dig a communication trench across
No Man's Land to speed the forward flow of reserves once the
German lines had been seized. The time of Zero hour was now
revealed: dawn, June 29th 1916.

The Fifth Leicesters were taken out of the line to practise their
assault just as the weather turned really foul. It was the wettest
June on record. At Fonquevillers, the recently cleared or newly
dug communication trenches – Derby Dyke, Roberts Avenue and
Crawl Boys Lane – flooded with water. When the Staffords and
Sherwood Foresters waded into the front line during a torrential
downpour on the night of June 28th, the mud in their assembly
positions reached up to their knees. A two-day drenching had
turned the battlefield into a quagmire. It seemed barely credible
that, heavily loaded as they were, the British would be expected
to attack in such conditions. They were not, for at the last minute
Zero was put back by 48 hours along the whole front. This raised
the question of what to do with the tens of thousands of tired,
muddy, over-burdened men who'd been assembled. The two
assault brigades of the 46th Division were withdrawn so that the
Corps Commander, General Snow, could watch them practise one
more time.

Soaked to the skin, the Staffords and Sherwood Foresters
marched the 10 miles back to Lucheux to perform for the generals.
As Milne remembers it, the château was perfectly appointed to suit
the brass hats' requirements:

There was a kitchen in which their unimpeachable chef could
exercise his culinary arts. There were comfortable bedrooms
fit for the reception of the tired limbs of Staff Officers when

the toil of the day was o'er. There was a quiet little room in which the orderlies played pontoon. There was a wine cellar . . .

Doubtless the Staff of the 46th Division did not stint General Snow (known to his men as 'Slush') at dinner that night, not on the eve of the biggest battle in history. Stint? Absolutely not. There was a job to be done and they were bloody well going to do it.

After their final practice, the Staffords and Sherwoods marched the 10 muddy miles back to Fonquevillers to do it for real. They were in position by midnight on June 30th, utterly exhausted. The Fifth Leicesters moved up and assembled in Midland Trench, a few hundred yards west of Fonquevillers church. Walter was in cellars with the rest of 'D' Company; he would be in the ninth wave, going over the top behind the Staffords.

In spite of its proximity to the front line, the village of Fonquevillers remained relatively intact on the eve of battle. Scraps of roof clung to the occasional upright wall, while the church tower – bearing the date 1683 in iron scrollwork – yet defied the German gunners with a clock face showing a permanent 11.45. The Leicesters had never held such a cushy bit of the front; there was even a YMCA canteen where two white-haired veterans dispensed tea and cakes. The place was known throughout the Army as Funky Villas.

On the triangular sward in front of the restored brick church my wife and I unpacked our picnic of cheese and ham. This was where the Staffords and Sherwood Foresters had halted for their last cigarettes in safety. Walter, too, had passed this way, filing down the narrow lane that led from the site of Midland Trench to where the Staffords assembled for the attack.

Brick walls gave way to small fields and pocket orchards tangled with the vines of deepest summer. The only people I met were two boys on one bicycle. A not-unpleasant smell of manure hung over the little military cemetery where Walter's comrades slept: Jimmy Allen, Military Medal, one of 'D' Company's bravest bombers, blown up by a howitzer shell; Lance-Corporal Stan Smith, another Hinckley lad, killed in action at the age of 21; and young Palmer, George Thomas Palmer, whose parents, James and Harriett, of 10 Infirmary Road, Leicester, never got over him being snuffed out so suddenly so far from home: 'Will some kind hand in a foreign land/Place a flower on my son's grave.'

Hills says the crypt of the church was used as a bomb store. On my way past I stooped to call through a broken fanlight. This was where Sergeant Goodman had looked after the Mills grenades and Stokes mortars, the scene of many a furtive loading and unloading. Further on, past Fonquevillers civilian cemetery, the lane forked at the Calvary Cross. Like many on the Western Front, it had survived repeated bombardments with apparently miraculous immunity:

As they passed by [says Milne], the more academic officers would say to one another, 'Strange, isn't it?' And the less erudite Private soldiers would grunt, 'Damned funny it never gets hit.' But some there were who, as they gazed, suddenly remembered the words of a certain company commander nineteen hundred years before: 'Surely this was the Son of God.'

It was impossible to tell if the present-day cross of iron was the self-same crucifix which had once inspired Milne's academic officers. It looked old enough and battered enough, and the angle at which the gabled Jesus leaned against the thorns suggested the quirk of authenticity. On July 1st 1916, all paths had led the same way.

I opened my trench map and took my bearings. Overhead,

as at the Hohenzollern Redoubt, sagged the black cables of an electricity transmission line, its pylons marching in giant strides along the exact route of the British Front. Behind me was Fonquevillers. Down in the shallow valley was No Man's Land. Facing me, along the top of a slightly steeper and higher slope, brooded Gommecourt Wood, where the Germans were waiting.

At 0624 hours, July 1st 1916, the British gunners discharged the final instalment of their preparatory barrage, a combination of high explosive and smoke calculated to cause maximum discomfiture to those of the enemy who might have survived the previous week of bombardment. The men in the British line had never experienced anything like it; they felt the bombardment through the soles of their boots. Those on the firestep saw the trees of Gommecourt Wood being hurled in the air like matchsticks. In the final minutes, trench mortars joined in to thicken the smoke still further and Gommecourt Wood disappeared in a boiling cloud of flame.

At 0730 hours, the whistles blew and the two leading waves of Sherwood Foresters – who had left their waterlogged trenches under cover of the barrage – stood up and formed a line at the bottom of the slope. A line of Staffords formed up to the right of them. After the deluge, the sky was bright and clear. The battalions went forward into No Man's Land at the steady pace they had practised so often. As the second wave cleared the last of the British wire, the third wave climbed out of their trenches to form up behind.

Four waves of Sherwoods crossed the shallow valley at two miles per hour, rifles at the port and bayonets glinting in the sun. As ordered, there was no cheering, just the occasional bark of command as NCOs kept their men in step. According to Hills, the first two waves cleared No Man's Land without loss. Some of them were drunk, having by an administrative error received twice their intended rum ration. They kept formation, however, crossed the flattened German front line and disappeared unscathed into the smoke at the edge of Gommecourt Wood. Then, as the fifth line of Robin Hoods set off, the wind freshened and the smoke rolled away, exposing the whole attack to German view.

On the extreme left flank of the British attack was an angle of German trenches known as 'The Z'. It stuck into No Man's Land like a spur and offered a perfect enfilade of the ground to be covered by the British assault, which is why it had been a priority target for the preparatory barrage. 'The Z' was meant to have been obliterated. Within minutes, its machine guns were wreaking slaughter. The Sherwoods were stopped dead in their tracks and the whole assault began to disintegrate.

Impressive as the British barrage had seemed, it hadn't done the job. The Germans had dug in too deeply to be hurt. As the leading waves of Sherwood Foresters advanced into the smoke-wreathed wreckage of Gommecourt Wood, the Germans burrowed up from their hiding-places and fell on them from behind. While the Sherwoods had been practising their attack at Lucheux, the Germans had been practising just as hard to repulse them. By the time the attack came, German machine-gunners were trained to get from their dugouts to the firestep in three minutes flat, with their guns assembled and ready to fire.

With the leading Sherwoods cut off, and with their support waves pinned down by enfilade fire, the left wing of the 46th Division attack degenerated into a bloody shambles. Officers gone, communications non-existent, unable to advance or retreat, the Robin Hoods curled up in shell-holes while the German artillery lashed them with shrapnel.

On the right flank, parallel to a short lane which had once connected Fonquevillers to Gommecourt village, the attack of the Staffords had gone even more badly. The first wave had barely crossed No Man's Land before it ran into trouble. The German machine guns shredded the Staffords as they floundered in the uncut barbed wire or bunched together to get through gaps. Many fell at the Sucrerie, a wrecked sugar-beet factory in the middle of No Man's Land. As the leading Staffords faltered, those behind were naturally drawn to the illusory prospect of shelter offered by the tumbled walls. It was a death trap. Every German gun and rifle knew the range of the Sucrerie to the inch. And yet it was here – into the storm of shrapnel and shot around the Sucrerie – that Captain Ward Jackson led two platoons of Fifth Leicesters to dig a communication trench:

> They started work and actually marked out their trench [says Hills], but their task was impossible. Capt. Ward Jackson, hit in the back and shoulder and very badly wounded, was only saved by Serjt. Major Hill, who pluckily carried him out of the fight. Seeing that the attack had failed, 2nd Lieut. Hepworth ordered the party back to our lines, where they found the rest of the battalion in the support lines and communication trenches, waiting for the Staffordshires to move forward.

After two months of practise and preparation, the battle had reached its critical phase inside the first few minutes. The Staffords had been checked with terrible losses, but the Sherwoods had made an entry. The success of the operation would be judged by how effectively the 46th and 56th Divisions could join hands to isolate Gommecourt; it was imperative to restore momentum. I holstered my trench map and charged.

I headed for 'The Z', where all the trouble was coming from. I galloped downhill at full throttle, kicking up dust, thrilled at the rush of speed in my face until I began to lose my balance, losing it completely where the downhill slope flattened out. My bag bumped awkwardly behind me like a spare pair of buttocks. I stumbled forward. I sprawled on my hands and knees, spectacles gone, nose down in the sharp corn-stalks, arse up in No Man's Land – like some idiot that I wouldn't want to be associated with.

At full tilt, it took a moderately unfit 39-year-old man with a bad knee 50 seconds to charge from the British line to 'The Z'. That was on a sunny afternoon with a slightly favourable tail wind. The time it would take to cover the same ground burdened with rifle, shovel and full pack would be . . . three minutes? Four? It was irrelevant. The British infantry had not been racing. The British generals had not allowed themselves to believe that there might be any Germans left to race against. The British attack of July 1st was planned as a walk-over, not a dash for victory.

'The Z' was a horrible place. It made me feel sick to look along the shallow valley through the eyes of the German machine-gunners. They couldn't have missed if they'd tried. It was murder: they simply opened up over flattened sights and the British walked straight into it, like a crowd leaving a football match.

Hundreds of Sherwoods and Staffords walked into the valley and kept on coming, row after row, just as they'd practised. Gommecourt Wood still reeked of it, despite the cheery twit and rustle of thrushes in the undergrowth. The wood's speckled glades, pitted with mossed craters and the ivy-wrapped remains of trenches, were sacred to the Sherwood Foresters.

I limped back to Fonquevillers via the Sucrerie. Its square foundations still formed a discernible impress in the grass, though no one who wasn't looking for it would know it was there. I checked my bearings. In fact, it was all still there – the place where the Leicesters tried to dig their trench; where the plucky Sergeant-Major rescued his wounded officer; where the Staffords had crawled, bleeding and blinded, through the flaming gates of

Hades. Back at Fonquevillers village green, I found my family playing French cricket, barefoot.

The car wouldn't start, not even the glimmer of a spark. I thought it might be a flat battery, due to excessive use of the air-conditioner. I almost felt pleased, since it vindicated my decision to spend money we didn't have on joining an international rescue organisation. I called them from Fonquevillers' public phone box and a pan-European network of highly trained professionals promised that a mechanic would be with us within an hour.

We nibbled the unconsumed portion of our day's rations and watched our shadows lengthen across the grass. Paunchy men played boules in the gravel near Fonquevillers' restored church, an ugly building in the same pseudo-Nouveau style as all the other post-War churches on the Somme. Dust motes spangled the slanting beams of the sun, silver boules clack-clacked, the smell of someone's barbecue wafted over a garden hedge, my children practised somersaults.

The car was a goner. Napoo. It was not the battery, it was the alternator. *'Kaput! Fini!'* said the mobile mechanic with Gallic indifference. Another summer evening settled peacefully on Funky Villas; we were stranded on the battlefield.

After supper at 'Billy's Billet' I joined the other guests in William's kit-built conservatory. Mr and Mrs Middlethorpe were just passing through, but Del from Manchester was a regular visitor who lived on the dole in between scavenging the battlefields for trophies. His pals among the French farmers kept things for him, and every couple of months he crossed the Channel to trade.

Mr Middlethorpe said he'd found some shrapnel balls at Thiepval. 'Once you start looking you can't stop.'

Del snorted unkindly. He slept in a caravan in William's barn, surrounded by chicken shit and battle scrap and empty beer bottles.

He went out before dawn each morning with only the butt of his cigar for breakfast. Del wouldn't give you half a fart for a fistful of shrapnel. Bayonets, that's where the action was. Bayonets, grenades, shell fuses, cap badges. Something solid or brassy.

'Collectors, they want something they can polish,' said Del.

I lingered after the others had gone to bed, worried about the financial implications of the burnt-out alternator. Our international rescue organisation had supplied a replacement vehicle – a tinny Renault – but our friendly *méchanicien*, Monsieur Alain Recherbe, had been unable to find a new part in his garage and couldn't say how long it would take to get one. I took a turn around William's garden and breathed deeply on the dewy scent of harvest. I stood in No Man's Land under a big yellow moon and knelt to feel the ground. An owl hooted, a net curtain gestured from the open window where my children slept. Back indoors, I sat up late with William's archive of Great War videos. The pale battalions marched to their destiny. Was Walter among them? Was I?

It was easier to follow the Fifth Leicesters on the Somme than in The Salient. The relentless spread of bricks and mortar around modern Ypres had interfered with the legibility of the terrain as an influence on battle. On the uplands of the Somme and the Ancre, however, there had been no need to continue building once the pre-War jigsaw of roads and fields had been reassembled. The post-War decline in the rural population of France had removed the need for new construction. What was restored on the Somme had therefore been preserved. The features which had been incorporated in the trench lines – buildings, tracks, ditches, hedges – were reconstituted after the War exactly as they had been before. My trench maps related to the landscape in front of me with astounding congruence.

If terrain governs tactics, the British tactics at Gommecourt were incredibly stupid. The distance between the British lines at Fonquevillers and the German lines at Gommecourt Wood was about 400 yards. On the south side of the Salient, along the line attacked by the 56th Division, the widest separation was about 800 yards. In both places, the British had to advance downhill into a shallow valley and up the other side before closing with the enemy. In both places, the British attack led across open ground enfiladed by enemy machine guns and artillery. It was the kind of proposition to make any prudent commander balk at frontal assault. After nearly two years of digging, the strength of the German fortifications demanded a full-blown siege or, failing that, a lightning barrage followed by infiltration, preferably under cover of darkness. The battle plan adopted by the British – an infantry advance at walking pace in broad daylight – was suicidal without an annihilating artillery barrage to precede it . . . which is what the British infantry didn't get.

The problem was not the literal weight of the bombardment. The British guns at the Somme fired some 20,000 tons of metal at the Germans in the seven days leading up to July 1st – a total of 1,627,824 individual shells, according to the *Official History* – but they were the wrong sort of shells. Only high-explosive was any good at smashing deep trenches, and the British didn't have enough. About three-quarters of the shells fired at the German positions were shrapnel, useless for dealing with emplacements and barbed wire unless very accurately fused.

To the British infantry, the bombardment looked like Hell. But chalk is soft, and much of the explosive power of the barrage was cushioned or dissipated. Added to which, an alarming proportion of the British shells – perhaps one-third – were duds. They exploded inside their guns, their drive bands snapped, they fell short, they fell wide, their fuses fell off. They failed.

And if the ordnance was deficient, so too was the standard

of gunnery. Among the pre-War officers of the Royal Field Artillery there had been a fashionable contempt for ballistics. Distances, angles and mathematics were for the swots of the Garrison Artillery. Horses were the thing for an Army chap, not guns. What was the point of trying to shoot at something you couldn't see? The result of this attitude was a crippling lack of seasoned bombardiers. It was accepted that the crew of a 1916 howitzer would need 100 shots to be sure of hitting their target. Such inaccuracy meant that it was deemed unsafe for the artillery to fire at anything within 300 yards of their own men; which is why there was no 'creeping barrage' for the British infantry on July 1st, whereas the French infantry to the south were shepherded forward by a barrage that preceded them by only 60 yards.

The clumsiness of the gunners, compounded by the huge delays in communication, made it impossible for the British to respond quickly once the attack of July 1st began to go wrong. After the opening barrage lifted from the German lines to allow the British infantry to advance, it could not be called back quickly enough to organise a second assault. The efforts of the 46th Division to regain momentum after their first attack was repulsed were partly hampered by the fact that it took four hours to arrange a new bombardment.

At 0800 hours, July 1st 1916, the British position at Gommecourt was still tenable . . . in theory. The first waves of Staffords had been savaged, but the Sherwoods had got through and, as far as anyone could tell, they were still battling towards their rendezvous with the 56th Division. Half an hour had been allowed for this link-up in the battle plan; if the Sherwoods could be supported quickly enough, a genuine breakthrough might yet be achieved. 'An attempt was therefore made to re-organize at once for another attack,' says Hills, 'but this was found to be impossible.'

In theory, the attack could have been re-started. In practice, 'this was found to be impossible.'

By 0900 hours the commander of the Staffords, Brigadier-General Williams, knew what that euphemism meant. Those of his men who'd survived the first assault were refusing to move. They'd had enough. They didn't recognise the battle they were fighting; it wasn't the one for which they'd practised so hard. The Germans hadn't been killed; their machine guns hadn't been knocked out; their wire hadn't been cut. The leading Staffords had been shot down like dogs. The only officers left were tearful kids. No one knew what was going on. Corporals and sergeants bellowed orders, but no one listened. It was insanity, another bloody Hohenzollern. The Staffords shut their eyes, blocked their ears and huddled with their wounded in the mud.

It got worse. Just when the need for clear and decisive command was paramount, it collapsed. Before the battle, the Staff of the 46th Division had arranged a traffic system for the communication trenches. 'Up' lines were for taking forward supplies and reserves; 'down' lines were for the evacuation of casualties and prisoners. At the crucial moment these orders were countermanded, with the result that nobody knew which lines were 'up' and which were 'down'. Carrying parties, stretcher-bearers, runners, walking wounded all tangled together and stuck fast in the cloying mud. And all the while, the German artillery kept pounding overhead with merciless, pre-registered accuracy.

Brigadier Williams, who'd been in charge of the Staffords for less than a month, shouted for someone to do something and sent two of his Staff forward. In the heaving confusion of the trenches the only battalion commander they could find was Colonel Jones of the Fifth Leicesters. They told him that the artillery was being called back for another shoot; his job was to get the men into four waves for a new attack.

This was not perhaps the most auspicious moment in that schoolmaster's military career. Leading the Fifth Leicesters must have been daunting enough in that inferno, without the extra burden of broken and demoralised Staffords being thrust upon him. To attack again was to invite a massacre, and all the men knew it. The General Officer Commanding 46th Division, Major-General the Hon. Edward Montagu-Stuart-Wortley C.B., C.M.G., D.S.O., M.V.O., took charge personally in order to see that it was carried out. He ordered a combined assault by what was left of the two brigades – Sherwoods on the left, Staffords and Fifth Leicesters on the right. It would be a repeat of the morning's attack, since that was what everybody had practised. The renewed advance would begin at 1215 hours, preceded by an artillery barrage and smoke.

At 1215 hours the attack was postponed because Colonel Jones and the Staffords weren't ready. As Hills explains:

> The men had been too well trained in their particular duties. A private soldier who has been told every day for a month that his one duty will be to carry a box of bombs to point Q, cannot readily forget that, and take an efficient part in an ordinary, un-rehearsed attack.

At 1315 hours the advance was postponed again. The Sherwoods hadn't been able to find any smoke bombs, and they declined to advance without them.

At 1445 hours another Zero passed. Still no smoke bombs for the Sherwoods. The traffic jam in the choked communication trenches had not been cleared, nor had the German artillery fire slackened. The mud in the British trenches had turned red.

At 1520 hours, enough Stokes mortar bombs had been scraped

together for a smoke-screen. The attack was now confirmed for 1530 hours. Walter fixed his bayonet to his muddy rifle and prepared as best he could for certain death.

At 1530 hours the British artillery opened up on the German front line, and the smoke was laid down. It was reasonably thick in front of the Staffords and Leicesters, but in front of the Sherwoods it consisted of just twenty bombs, producing barely enough smoke to screen more than a few yards. Twenty men on the left climbed from their trench into a hail of German machine-gun fire; two crawled back to the parapet. Brigadier Shipley ordered the rest to stay put. Seeing that the Sherwoods were staying put, the Staffords and Leicesters also stayed put. The smoke-screen drifted away; its only effect had been to alert the Germans to the imminence of a new attempt against them for, as the smoke thinned, so the Germans laid down another heavy shrapnel barrage on the British front lines. It was at precisely this moment that the British barrage lifted from the German line in anticipation that the infantry were about to reach it. Conditions were absolutely perfect for another slaughter of British infantry.

The attack was cancelled. The Corps Commander, General Snow, learning that the 56th Division had finally been ejected from its last footholds south of Gommecourt, called the whole show off. His planned pincer movement had failed utterly. The troops of both divisions had been knocked senseless and would have to be replaced, and that would take hours. It wasn't worth a second effort; it wasn't worth the reserves. As far as diverting the Germans was concerned, VII Corps of the Third Army had surely done enough.

The generals were too stupid, the men were too brave. It was the politicians behind the scenes, interfering with strategy. It was the French, changing their plans up to the very last minute.

It was the constant rain. It was the useless artillery. Everybody and everything was to blame for the disaster of July 1st 1916.

'It was Haig,' said Del. 'I hate the bastard!'

Del took it personally. The great Somme myth was part of his patrimony. At Zero hour 150,000 men went over the top; 57,000 had been killed or wounded by nightfall. The only place where the British captured and held any ground was in the south, where the French – better trained, more experienced, tactically canny – took all their objectives and dragged the British forward on their coat-tails.

'It was the greatest act of murder,' said William, 'that was ever perpetrated against the English working man.'

It sounded like a quote. Crackpots and conspiracists are drawn to the apocalyptic vastness of the Somme and the scope it offers for disputation: Haig the Stalwart; Haig the Butcher. Haig the Stupid; Haig the Seer. Haig the Anal Retentive Mediocrity with an Impaired Achievement-Motivation; Haig the Eventually Triumphant Through Loyalty to the Values of His Race.

'Haig!' snarled Del. 'If Haig were to walk through that door now, I'd spit on him!'

Del and William were Kitchener boys. Del was mad about the 36th Division, the Ulsters; William was a lifelong fan of the Thirsty Firsts, the 31st Division, the Pals. Del's home ground was Thiepval; William's was Serre. As an honorary Hinckley Terrier – 'We mind our manners, we spend our tanners' – I felt barely qualified to offer an opinion. As far as Haig's culpability for the Somme débâcle was concerned, I didn't have strong opinions. Since Haig was learning on the job, like all the other generals trying to deal with mass armies in formation, it was inevitable that mistakes would be made, and that – given the sheer size of the armies engaged – casualties would be enormous. Haig, as Commander-in-Chief, must take part of the blame for what happened, but so must Rawlinson. It was Sir Henry Rawlinson, as Commander of the Fourth Army, who decreed that the assault of July 1st should be a walk not a run. He it was who decreed that there should be a long, pulverising bombardment rather than a short, surprising one.

The *Official History* concedes – in so far as such a concession was possible – that the operation at Gommecourt was a fiasco:

It seems improbable that G.H.Q. realized the strength – and that strength enormously increased by flanking artillery defence – of the Gommecourt Salient. If an attack is to be made merely to hold enemy troops and prevent their employment elsewhere, a weak or vulnerable part of the enemy's front should be chosen, not the strongest. Further, Gommecourt was particularly easy of defence, and from the shape of the ground it was a most difficult place from which to disengage troops in the event of partial failure or incomplete success.

If Gommecourt was the strongest position on the 14-mile front that the British planned to attack, then Haig stands accused of negligence. Why didn't he 'realise' the strength of the Gommecourt Salient? Because he didn't ask? Because General Headquarters didn't check? The *Official History* insinuates that the Corps Commander at Gommecourt, 'Slushy' Snow, exceeded his brief in attempting to take the position:

It must be distinctly borne in mind that in Sir Douglas Haig's plan nothing depended on the capture of Gommecourt ... There was no intention of exploiting the capture of Gommecourt by sending a force southwards from the village to roll up the German line . . . No troops were provided or available for such a purpose . . . A success at Gommecourt would merely shorten the British line by cutting off an enemy salient.

The officially historicised version of the Haig plan was the exact opposite of what the Fifth Leicesters had been led to believe:

> Our action on the 1st was failure [says Hills]. This cannot be denied. The retaining of enemy troops on our front was done by our Artillery and other preparation, and the extra German Division was lured into the line opposite us at least three days before the battle. Our assault made not the slightest difference to this. Our object on the 1st was to capture Gommecourt, and this we failed to do.

Two days after the battle, General Snow sent a message to his troops congratulating them for the way they had 'fought and endured'. He was aware, he wrote, that many gallant acts had been performed: 'Although Gommecourt has not fallen into our hands, the purpose of the attack, which was mainly to contain and kill Germans, was accomplished.'

Total casualties among the 46th and 56th Divisions at Gommecourt amounted to 6,531 officers and men killed, missing or wounded. Total German casualties amounted to 1,241, including those killed in the week-long preparatory bombardment. The casualty figures for officers were particularly disproportionate: the British lost 103 officers killed; the Germans lost 12.

Hills writes:

> It is comparatively easy to criticise after the event, but there

were one or two obvious reasons for the failure which were apparent to all. The rapid dispersal of the smoke barrage, the terrible enfilade bombardment from the left ['The Z'] consequent on the inactivity of the Division [the 37th] on our left, the failure of our Artillery to smash up German posts, and in some cases German wire, and, perhaps the fact that our preparations were so obvious that the Boche was waiting for us. But in the face of all this, fresh troops in ideal conditions might have succeeded. Ours were tired after their journey to Lucheux and back, had had to live several nights in hopelessly foul and waterlogged trenches, and, so far from fresh, were almost worn before they started to attack.

The remnants of the Stafford Brigade were ordered out of the line at 1600 hours, July 1st 1916. The Fifth Leicesters took over from the Staffords, while the Sherwoods were replaced by the Lincolns. The forward trenches at Fonquevillers were in a horrific condition. Bodies and parts of bodies had been trampled into the mud, limbs protruded from where dugouts and trenches had collapsed, the tattered accoutrements of annihilated battalions lay strewn over No Man's Land like a picnic that had gone horribly wrong. Out there, among the craters and shell-holes, a khaki sleeve or trouser-leg twitched occasionally amongst the ranks of the fallen. Dying men keened piteously in the extremity of their suffering. After a day of glorious summer, daylight clung on in the west. Not until 2200 hours did darkness fall, allowing the first wraiths to crawl back to Funky Villas.

The Leicesters worked throughout the night and into the next day collecting the wounded. The Germans offered a truce at dawn on July 2nd after running up a Red Cross banner over their trenches. Walter went out to scavenge for wounded under the eyes of the enemy. The dead were left where they'd fallen.

'There was ceremonial saluting on both sides,' says the *Official History*, 'but no fraternization.'

Neither Hills nor Milne mentions this gesture. Both, perhaps, were too traumatised to be impressed by old-fashioned courtesies. Milne's account of the battle stutters with repressed rebellion and rage:

> Gommecourt is attacked on July 1st. The attack fails. The 4th Leicesters are reserve battalion of the reserve brigade. They are not sent to the slaughter. The Staffords and Sherwoods lose heavily. The taps of the Somme blood bath are full on.

The squandering of the New Armies on July 1st set new standards of British military incompetence. The magnitude of the failure seemed exactly inverse to the exalted expectations which had preceded it. This was especially true at those places, like Gommecourt, where not a single inch of ground had been gained. The men of the 46th Division knew they'd been sacrificed to no purpose. Their officers knew it, Sir Douglas Haig knew it. Everyone looked for someone else to blame. Haig's authorised biographers, Dewar and Boraston, blamed Major-General Montagu-Stuart-Wortley for creating the traffic jam in the 46th Division's communication lines: 'The failure of the subsidiary attack must be ascribed, in part at least, to the faulty handling of the supporting troops of the Division.'

This 'faulty handling' of the 46th Division was made more ignominious by inevitable comparison with the performance of the 56th Division, attacking simultaneously from the opposite side of the Gommecourt salient. 'That Division,' says the *Official History*, 'had by careful preparations and a fine advance attained nearly all of its principal objectives.'

The 56th (1st London) Division was a Territorial formation

like the 46th. But whereas the 46th comprised the artisans and factory-fodder of the industrial Midlands, the 56th consisted of glamour regiments like the London Scottish, the Queen Victoria's Rifles, the Queen's Westminster Rifles and the 13th County of London, the Kensingtons. The London Scottish had been the first Territorial regiment to see action on the Western Front and, like many of its sister battalions in the 56th Division, it included some of the smartest brains of the Imperial metropolis – journalists, lawyers, teachers, civil servants, and the occasional young blade with connections to the very highest reaches of the Establishment. When three-quarters of these men became casualties in a single day, the whole of London heard about it.

'The assault of the 56th Division was carried out with the greatest dash,' says the *Official History*, 'and the failure to capture the Gommecourt salient cannot in any way be attributed to the gallant regiments composing it, for they did practically all that was asked of them.' By 0930 hours, the time by which the Sherwoods and Staffords had been broken beyond recall, the Londoners had taken three lines of trenches and were sending back prisoners. Some were even supposed to have reached point 'X' for the rendezvous with the 46th Division.

That was the limit of their success, however. The Germans, having wiped out the Thirsty Firsts at Serre, diverted artillery fire from there to Gommecourt. Just as the 46th Division was enfiladed by artillery from the left, so the 56th Division found itself enfiladed from the right. The German barrage fell like a curtain of steel across No Man's Land, cutting off the Londoners from support and reinforcement. Thus isolated, they were systematically bombed out of their lodgments. As the day wore on, the Londoners' signals from the German trenches flickered more and more feebly. The flash of rifle-fire and bomb explosions abated as the last diehards went down fighting or surrendered. By 1600 hours, the Germans were back in possession of their battered front line and what was left of the pride of London was crawling back to Hebuterne.

That was the story up and down the British line. The New-foundlanders had been wiped out at Hamel; the Durhams at Ovillers; the Green Howards at Fricourt; the Tyneside Scottish at La Boiselle; the Ulsters at Thiepval ... Each strongpoint in the German line had been a particular Gehenna for some British regiment. 'We had heard of partial and complete failures in other parts of the line,' wrote Siegfried Sassoon, 'and the name of Gommecourt had already reached us with ugly implications.'

The breakdown of casualties between the divisions engaged at Gommecourt was as follows: Londoners – 4,314 officers and men killed, wounded, missing or captured. North Midlanders – 2,455 officers and men killed, wounded, missing or captured.

In gross terms, the 56th Division appeared to have tried almost twice as hard as the 46th to carry out General Snow's orders. In looking for a scapegoat for the débâcle, it was therefore comparatively easy for General Snow to decide which of his divisional commanders to sacrifice.

The precise circumstances surrounding the departure of Major-General the Hon. E.J. Montagu-Stuart-Wortley, C.B., C.M.G., D.S.O., M.V.O. are not alluded to directly in the written sources. Hills says simply that the Major-General 'went back to England'. Milne says he 'relinquished command'. Neither expresses any personal sense of regret. It must be some kind of indictment, however, that during two years under his command neither Hills nor Milne had found cause to express a warm or respectful word about him.

The tragedy of Gommecourt arises from the discrepancy between the bravery of the men and the ineptitude of their commanders. The idea behind the Big Push was that the combined generalship of the various Staffs – Army, Corps, Division, Brigade

– would save the men unnecessary risks and steer them to victory. The actual story of the Somme battle, as it developed into a Verdun-style grind of attrition, was vice-versa: it was the loyalty and endurance of the troops, dying in their tens of thousands, that saved the reputations of the Staffs. Two thousand Englishmen lay dead at Gommecourt on the night of July 1st because of the inability of their commanders to make a professional job of 'drawing away German reserves'. First-hand Intelligence and practical advice from regimental officers in the trenches had been ignored, and their helpful suggestions dismissed. The best glimpse of General Montagu-Stuart-Wortley comes from a soldier who didn't serve under him, Dick Read, a machine-gunner in the Eighth Leicesters. On the eve of battle, Read was with a working party just north of Fonquevillers, carrying Stokes mortar bombs up to the front line:

On the way back, we met some 4th Leicestershire Terriers of the 46th Division. They told us they were going over the top the next morning at Gommecourt. A few hundred yards further on we passed a motor car in which sat a general, talking to two staff officers. The sargeant in charge of us dutifully made us march to attention and 'eyes left'. It was said the general commanded the 46th Division . . . As we passed the car, we saw to our amazement that the general was holding up two little toy dogs for the officers' inspection. Both had light blue silk ribbon bows round their necks. Many were the bitter comments made as we plodded on back. His seemed to be a different war from ours. In after years, I think that perhaps his little dogs may have helped him to keep his sanity when faced with the hell that followed shortly after we saw him.

★　　★　　★

Bruce Chatwin's book, *The Songlines*, explores the belief of Australian aborigines that Reality is brought into being by Song. The aborigine, as he follows his ancestors' footprints through the outback, 'sings up' the landscape they inhabited. His songs recreate watercourses and rocks by echoing the original songs of creation, before which all was a dream. The 'songline' pertaining to any given tract of territory is a map and direction-finder to the singer. It is also a title deed, a proof of ownership, a sign of belonging.

I was as happy as a lark in No Man's Land, singing up the spirits of my ancestors, asserting my Great War inheritance. I crossed and re-crossed the front lines with impunity, breasted the wire without harm. No one bothered me. The farmers around Gommecourt seemed used to the sight of an occasional Englishman falling out of a hedge without warning. I respected their '*Chasse Réservée – Entrée Interdite*' signs (unless I thought no one was looking) and never walked through standing crops. If in doubt, I would look down at my feet for physical evidence, and if I found shrapnel balls or shell fragments I took them as confirmation that I was on the right lines.

In Gommecourt Wood I chatted to the sons and grandsons of trees that Walter must have known. I found clutches of rust-mottled shells, British duds, nestling in the sunken remains of German trenches. I looked long and hard at everything. This, I thought, was how it must have been. In all the Great War's accumulation of individual agonies, mountainous beyond measure, these details were among the common weal: blistered feet and tired limbs; insect bites; the tedium of watchfulness; the smell of the earth; hunger pangs. Death visited, singly or in scores, but life went on, somehow.

My French is bad, but better than the English of the angry man who intercepted me at one of Gommecourt Wood's rickety gates. He berated me for trespass, assuming that I was a trophy-hunter and that I had disturbed his game by truffling for something brassy in the undergrowth. He flicked at the strap of my knapsack. Who was I? What had I been doing? What had I got in my bag? I showed him a trench map.

'*Je suis un étudiant de La Guerre Mondiae. Mon grand-père était ici pour la bataille de la Somme avec l'Armée Britannique. Je n'ai prends rien, M'sieu.*'

Yes; I startled a deer while I was in the wood. Yes; I knowingly ignored the sign reading, '*Chasse Reservée – Entrée Interdite*'. I pointed towards Fonquevillers.

'*Devant là, étaient les boyaux Britanniques—*' I jerked my thumb over my shoulder. '*Dans le Bois de Gommecourt, étaient les Allemands—*'

I set the map for him and explained the pincer movement of the 46th and 56th Divisions on July 1st.

'*Tous les soldats Britannique sont morts pour Gommecourt. Milles de soldats. Kaput! Fini! Beaucoup de sang. Trop mal.*'

The angry man uttered a grunt of grudging acceptance. He explained again about *La Chasse*, but calmly this time. It was his livelihood, catching game and curing it. He ran a *charcuterie*. *Oui, oui. Bien sûr*. He couldn't have understood the satisfaction it gave me to shake hands with the butcher of Gommecourt.

Normally, as I've said, I try to avoid discussion of the Great War at the dinner table. My enthusiasm either disturbs people or bores them. At 'Billy's Billet' I felt that if I was not quite in the company of friends then I could at least be sure of a sympathetic hearing from fellow-sufferers of the same virus. We dined with the Ogilvies. The Middlethorpes had gone and Del was busy in the barn prior to an early-morning departure for the Davyhulme Jobcentre. I knew the Ogilvies were Australian before they'd said a word. Dale had the torso of a Greek god and long blond hair in a pony-tail. Sheila, his partner, had a chin like a brick and pale eyes set too close together. Neither of them had heard of Bruce Chatwin.

Halfway through their second helpings, Sheila asked, with a rasp of exasperation, if I didn't believe that anything of interest – apart from the Great War – had happened in the twentieth century. I told her that the only thing which came to mind was England's 4–2 victory over Germany in the 1966 World Cup.

'You Poms! You do realise it was us Australians that did all the dirty work for yer?'

'Yes,' I said. 'Thank you.'

Sheila had the irritating habit of ending her sentences with a rising inflection that turned every statement into a questioning chirrup. Her personal obsession with the Great War was the perfidy of Albion – how the British had exploited and abused their brave colonial cousins. It was the Australians who had won the War.

'Whenever the Poms had, like, a really serious problem to deal with, they sent for the Aussies. That's how they knew they would get the job done?'

'Mmmn.'

The Australian troops were notoriously relaxed about discipline, but they fought like hell. The average Aussie was taller and broader and stronger than his British counterpart, and in most cases he was a more natural fighter. A spirit of 'mateship' gave the Aussies an understanding in battle that the British reliance on drill often failed to inculcate.

'Pozières,' said Sheila. 'The bloody Poms let us down on that one, same as all the others?'

The village of Pozières – a Hooge-like collection of farms and outhouses on a long, straight road between Albert and Bapaume – was where the Australians were first sent into the Somme battle. Two British divisions had already failed to take the position when the first Australians were called up. It was another Gommecourt-style pincer movement: Aussies on the right; British on the left.

'Except, where were the Poms? Were they, like, on the left? No way. There was no one on the left except the Germans—'

The Territorials of the 48th (South Midland) Division did not distinguish themselves at Pozières on July 22nd 1916.

'Yeah,' I said. 'And what about Bellenglise?'

We were haggling now, like rival football fans. What about September 29th 1918? When the 46th (North Midland) Division burst through the Hindenburg Line and left the Aussies and the Yanks on their starting blocks?

'Sounds like a lie.'

The Leicesters crossed the canal and broke the German line while the Aussies were still at their breakfast.

'Cobblers!'

The Scots, the Irish and the Welsh all thought they had won the War. The Australians, the Canadians and the South Africans all thought they had won the War. The French thought they had won it. The Americans thought they had won it. The Germans refused to acknowledge that they had lost it. It was the British who won the War. They had help, the whole Empire helped, but in the end, after all rival claims have been objectively assessed, it should be emphasised clearly once and for all that it was the British who won the Great War. North Midlanders won the Great War at the Battle of Bellenglise on September 29th 1918.

July 1st 1916 was a calamity for the British nation. But it was only the first day of what developed into a four-month effort to break the German Army. Every time the Germans knocked them down, the British got up and attacked again. Yard by yard, trench by trench, village by village, they slogged their way forward. It may have begun as a push for a breakthrough but it was quickly converted into something else – not a battle for territory but a contest of will. Haig versus Falkenhayn; England versus Germany.

By the time the Battle of the Somme was shut down in November, it had cost the Germans something under 600,000 casualties. British and French losses combined were put at 614,000. The British dead were mourned as the flower of the nation's youth. The Germans mourned for the opposite reason: they had lost that core of battle-hardened NCOs and regular soldiers which had formed the backbone of their Army. Their numbers might be replaced, but not their accumulated battle lore and fighting spirit. The eventual German withdrawal to the Hindenburg Line in 1917 confirmed how much they had been weakened during 1916. The British had made the Somme untenable. As battles of attrition go, it was an Allied victory. Thus it was, as the Germans pulled back, that the Leicesters eventually came to liberate Gommecourt.

The 46th Division had been withdrawn in disgrace on July 3rd and sent north to a quiet stretch of line to pull itself together. General Montagu-Stuart-Wortley was replaced by a gunner called William Thwaites, the epitome of the Great War brass hat. Thwaites was short, fat, red-faced and, Milne says, nearly always in a rage:

> He believed there was no such thing as a perfect battalion. He once inspected our transport . . . the wagons were clean, the mules well groomed, the harness in perfect condition. Every buckle was fastened, every strap in place. He looked here, he looked there. At last he turned to the transport officer, who was rejoicing in secret, and with eyes blazing with wrath (real

or simulated) snorted, 'Why on earth can't you grow a proper moustache?'

General Thwaites' first inspection of the Fifth Leicesters, at their billets in Bailleulmont on July 13th, was thorough enough. Hills says he looked the men over carefully and scrutinised the officers with the eye of a connoisseur. But his introductory speech was a clanger. He got the name of the regiment wrong – calling them the Fifth Leicesters to their faces instead of the militarily correct 'Fifth Leicestershires' – and he addressed Lieutenant-Colonel Jones throughout as 'Colonel Holland'. These gaffes, says Hills, were never to be forgotten.

For seven months, the 46th Division held the five miles of line north of Fonquevillers and took no further part in offensive operations. Higher Command had decided that the Terriers of the North Midlands were not up to the job. They were fit only for garrison duties and were assigned the trenches opposite the German-held village of Monchy au Bois. The Leicesters mounted the occasional raid and withstood periodic shelling. It was dullish work but safe. No Man's Land was more than half a mile wide in parts of the sector, and the most persistent enemy turned out to be the weather.

First came the autumn mud, then one of the harshest winters in memory. Shovels bounced uselessly off the frozen earth; men woke up to find the water in their canteens frozen solid. They wore all their socks and all their vests all the time. They took their rations to bed with them so that the bread wouldn't freeze. Patrols venturing into No Man's Land wore white gowns to blend in with the snow.

Despite the punishing cold, the Leicesters developed something akin to affection for Monchy. Staying in the same place brought the comfort of civilian pleasures. Out of the line, the Leicesters were able to form normal relationships with the people of Bienvillers, Pommier and Souastre. Some aspects of trench life were made worse by the cold weather. The rat population increased enormously, and such German shelling as did occur sent up ragged chunks of frozen earth as deadly in their effects as shrapnel. But the solid ground also made movement to and from the front line much easier, enabling hot meals to be brought right up to the firestep.

As fresh drafts arrived, the depleted battalions of the 46th Division were gradually restored to full strength. The time-served men got their full leave allowance. By the end of 1916, the Officers' Mess of the Fifth Leicesters was complete for the first time since it had left England. As the regiment waxed fat, Lieutenant-Colonel Jones was inspired to eulogise in verse:

> D'you know our Monchy au Bois,
> So charming, so je ne sais quois,
> We've been there so long.
> And found it so bon,
> That we'd go back there any old fois.

On St Valentine's Day 1917, the thaw set in for real and with it came the first signs of a German withdrawal. As the trenches turned to mud again, the Fifth Leicesters were ordered south to their old lines directly opposite Gommecourt. On February 24th, patrols reported that they had heard the Germans shouting 'bonsoir'. On the 25th, they reported that Gommecourt Park appeared to have been evacuated; some German dugouts had been set on fire. On the night of the 26th, the Leicesters concentrated on wire-cutting. On February 27th, they entered the German lines in strength.

This was the first time, apart from the attack on the Hohenzollern Redoubt, that the Leicesters had been inside German trenches, and they were astounded by what they discovered. Some of the largest dugouts were 40 feet deep, equipped with electric lighting and kitchens. To Milne – accustomed to the black, stinking funk-holes which had passed for dugouts on the British side of No Man's Land – these dry, snugly furnished defences seemed almost palatial, and opposite Fonquevillers they were connected by a network of tunnels. Some led back to communication trenches in the rear; one led all the way to 'The Z', which explained how the Germans had been able to man that position so quickly after the British barrage lifted on July 1st. As the Leicesters fanned out to occupy Gommecourt, a German rearguard remained in 'The Z' to harass their forward patrols. Hills says the Germans sat at one end of the tunnel, the Leicesters at the other:

> 'There were many booby traps, such as loose boards exploding a bomb when trodden on; trip wires at the bottom of dugout steps bringing down the roof; and other infernal machines. We were warned of these and had no casualties . . . Our bombing parties were very vigorous, and in one case consumed the hot coffee and onions left by a party [of Germans] disturbed at breakfast.

In front of Gommecourt church I felt the ghost of something missing. The village was different from its close neighbours, Fonquevillers and Hebuterne, and not just because it was smaller. Its restored church was of the same perfunctory design, thrown up with the same post-War haste and inattention to detail, but it was bleaker somehow, more cynical. Over the road, where the passing stranger might have expected to find a municipal garden or a few benches to provide a communal focus for the village, there was an absence.

The heart of Gommecourt had been torn out, replaced by a

sorry patch of broken pasture where the Germans had dug the Kern Redoubt. Thirty or forty feet below ground lay unknown, evil things. Gommecourt had sealed up its secrets, but it remained blighted. The village war memorial, unlike those in Fonquevillers and Hebuterne, bore the names of victims as well as heroes – civilians who had been tortured and murdered during the German occupation of 1914–1917. Hills recounts:

> The French were immensely pleased at regaining part of their lost territory, though it was a pathetic sight to see some of the old people coming to look at the piles of bricks which had once been their homes. Two ladies came to Gommecourt with a key, little thinking that – so far from finding a lock – they would not even find a door or door-way. There was not even a brick wall more than two feet high.

If it had not been for the likes of Walter Butterworth, Gommecourt would today be a German village and its war memorial would tell a different tale. But Walter was not among the liberators, he was in hospital again. His Field Medical Card, stamped with the rubber-stamp of the 37th Casualty Clearing Station and dated February 1st 1917, identifies his condition as 'I.C.T. Scalp'. By the time Walter was received at the 26th General Hospital eleven days later, the diagnosis had been changed to 'Impetigo', a complaint characterised by pustules and flaking of the skin. After another four days, he was transferred again, this time to the 25th General Hospital, and his diagnosis was changed once more – to 'Seborrhoea', otherwise known as very bad dandruff. The doctor's notes on the obverse of Walter's case sheet (Army Form W.3162) record his progress under treatment:

Chronic condition – Seborrhoea scalp.
Scaly – no redness. Not acute.
Patch L. Knee.
23 Feb 1917, nearly well
2 Mar 1917, few small boils scalp
8/3/17, just well.
Discharged to Marlborough Camp for Special Leave.

When we went to the village of Avesnes le Comte to collect the car, Monsieur Recherbe led us into his office and wrote down a figure in francs which ended in three noughts. After translating this into pounds sterling, I realised that the new alternator was going to cost very nearly the same amount as I had paid for the car two years previously. Monsieur Recherbe shrugged sympathetically and offered me a cigarette in case – in the extremity of shock – I should want to start smoking. He prodded his invoice with a blunt finger: it was a genuine Honda part, all the way from Brussels. And plastic wouldn't do either. When it came to Englishmen in trouble, Monsieur Recherbe's terms were strictly cash.

We raised the money by withdrawing to our permitted maximum at every Visa-compatible bank within a four-mile radius. Our liquidity as a family unit evaporated in an instant. The holiday was over. There was no point in being bitter about it. There was no point expecting Alain Recherbe to be grateful that my grandad had suffered very bad dandruff to liberate France from German occupation. That's why wars are fought – so the survivors can fleece the victors under the banner of Liberty.

We drove back to 'Billy's Billet' trying to work out a plan . . . there was no plan. We packed in a hurry and paid Jess with an English cheque that I signed with my fingers crossed. The search for Walter was over for another year. I drove north to the Channel with furious concentration, praying that nothing else would burn out or drop off the car until we'd got to Blighty.

6

BLIGHTY

But there's no land like England, and no other gel like mine:
Thank Gawd for dear old Blighty in the mawnin'.

Robert Service, 'Going Home'

Very few soldiers spurned leave. The odd Regular regarded the idea as un-military – on the grounds that since soldiers were meant to fight, war was their natural element. Some men discovered stronger bonds of loyalty within their platoons than they had ever known at home, and so chose not to go. For the majority, however, leave was one of the few things that made the War endurable. Walter would certainly have been at the head of the queue when leave came round for the Fifth Leicesters once they'd begun to recover from the Battle of the Somme. Not only had he received a wound without reward at Vimy, but he was a married man with a son he hadn't seen, which placed him in a deserving category all of his own.

By late 1916, the British Army had systematised arrangements for leave as thoroughly as every other aspect of the infantryman's existence. Divisional Staffs allocated leave to brigades; brigades divided it between battalions; battalions served it up to company officers; officers doled it out to the men. Extenuating circumstances were rarely taken into account, and soldiers were only notified of their leave on the day it began. Receipt of leave triggered the immediate dash from the trenches of those concerned. Sometimes they barely even stopped to pack; everyone knew someone who knew someone who'd been killed with his leave chit still in his hand.

Chronologically, the distance between the duckboards of the front line and the gangplank of the leave ship was a matter of hours. Psychologically, it measured a lifetime. To survive trench warfare, men had to learn to divest themselves of their civilian virtues. Letters and parcels kept them in touch with loved ones and were treasured proof that they had not been forgotten. By 1916, the postal services of the British Army were handling 11 million letters a week and 875,000 parcels. But brooding over lost comforts could soften the resolve. It was better for men to keep their private thoughts private. 'Home' became a mythical place to which there were only three sure avenues of return: ultimate victory; a Blighty wound; leave. It might take a Jock from some remote glen two days or more to get home, but Walter was never more than a couple of train rides from his own front door.

At Leicester railway station the gas-lamps of Walter's day had gone, along with the first and second class refreshment rooms, the uniformed porters, the milk churns and the wicker baskets. Instead, a hoarding installed by the city council boasted that Thomas Cook, the founder of modern tourism, had organised his first excursion from Leicester station on July 5th 1841. My train to Hinckley was a brisk, loco-less affair crowded with Lincoln-to-Coventry folk and their cross-country shopping. It chugged through a tunnel, then stopped for no apparent reason. To the right lay the hospital where I was born and the gantries of the main stand at Filbert Street, home of Leicester City Football Club. To the left was the regional headquarters of British Gas. The patch of green in front of Leicester Prison had been renamed in honour of Nelson Mandela. 'Your freedom and mine cannot be separated. Leicester City Council – working for equality.'

In the days of Thomas Cook, Leicester made large quantities of hosiery, footwear and all kinds of useful machinery for the British Empire. Today it was making small quantities of hosiery and footwear, and working for equality. The city fathers wanted to portray Leicester as an enterprising place to do business with; what the railway revealed were the back-ends of builders' yards and windy housing schemes littered with supermarket trolleys. South Wigston station backed on to a correctional institution for young offenders surrounded by razor wire. After Narborough, we entered a semi-industrialised landscape of scrapyards and muddy farms. Traffic on the new motorway whizzed past a Chernobyl-sized industrial incinerator. Then, gently, the land began to fold in upon itself, disclosing glimpses of brooks and woods and manor houses that Walter would have recognised. Grey roofs clustered round church steeples. The fields grew greener, the livestock cleaner. This was the hallowed ground, the cradle of Walter's youth, the heartland.

Hinckley station seemed derelict and unwanted. A board over the window of the ticket office said, 'To Let'. In Walter's day the railway had been the artery for all the town's raw materials and finished goods. As soon as he'd set foot upon the platform, he would have known that business was booming. The air would have been thick with smoke and soot from the dozens of steam-engines that kept the power looms turning. Everyone was working overtime in 1916 to fulfil government contracts for the boots, socks and underwear that were the basis of Hinckley's prosperity.

The first pub in town was the Railway Hotel, a low, corner tavern where any returning soldier was guaranteed a free pint and a pat on the back. Here, Walter would have had his first taste of what the Great War meant for the drinking classes – weak ale, high prices, shorter hours. He would also have learned about high wages and fat profits. At a time when Walter was getting a shilling a day (plus separation allowance, plus child allowance), even unskilled workers in the boot and shoe trade were clearing thirty bob a week.

From the railway, Walter's route home would have taken him up Station Road past the Territorial Drill Hall, where he and the rest of 'D' Company had enlisted. The comfortable villas built by a previous generation of solicitors and doctors had long since been sub-divided and made ugly by decades of amateur conversions. The public lavatory opposite the Post Office displayed a 'Loo of the Year' award, which only emphasised the lack of a more substantial cause for civic pride. Too many of Hinckley's factories had fallen silent, too many of its shops were boarded up.

According to Uncle Peter, the Butterworth family residence during the Great War had been No. 3, King Street – a narrow terrace behind the Union Hotel in the centre of town. The site was too cramped to have been salubrious, but No. 3 was where Walter Noël Gordon had been born, and as such it was that piece of the *Patria* which Walter had volunteered to defend with his life. I stood outside it for a while with my mouth agape, feeling stupid. No. 3, King Street, and the houses on either side of it, had been turned into a nick-nack emporium. Why had I not anticipated such a let-down?

I crossed the road and looked dumbly at the window display. Of what possible value was this? I made a list: four-poster baby cribs with lemon silk curtains; photograph frames in fuchsia satin; female field-mice in milkmaid flounces; wickerwork letter racks; potpourris; corn dollies; chintz curtain pelmets; wooden ducks; Ali Baba linen baskets trimmed with lace; bundles of dried flowers tied with velvet; book-ends with field-mice motifs; botanical prints in distressed antique frames; porcelain figurines of Beatrix Potter characters ... I entered to ask directions to Hinckley's War Memorial. Potpourri fumes whooshed through the door, stinging my eyes. A woman with big hair and scarlet lips came out to serve me. She was sorry she couldn't help; the visitor information bureau was in the town library. When I got there, of course, it was shut and I had to inquire elsewhere.

After the Norman conquest of 1066, the land around Hinckley was given to the Lord High Steward of England, the last of whom was King Henry IV. The highest hill of the demesne was crowned with a palisade and surrounded by a deep ditch known as a fosse. Such wooden forts served as precursors of the formidable castles with which the Normans subjugated the Anglo-Saxons. Hinckley was never that important, its castle remained unbuilt. But the mound and ditch survived, and the track up to them evolved over the centuries into Castle Street, the town's commercial axis. When the time came in 1919 to consider where to commemorate those townsmen who'd died in the Great War, Castle Mound was still regarded as the historic and symbolic heart of Hinckley.

The top of the mound was scooped out in the manner of a shallow amphitheatre. At one end, approached by a flight of steps, a stone wall was built, bearing six bronze tablets inscribed with the names of The Fallen. They were arrayed in alphabetical order, Abbot to Young, without distinction of rank or military honour. There were six Moores, no Butterworths. The place where Walter would have been – after the Butler boys and before P. Carter –

was empty. I placed my fingers between the lines and touched the dizzying possibility of my own non-existence. If Walter's name had been there, I would not . . .

In the centre of the arena, on an octagonal dais, stood a column surmounted by a female figure. She looked down with her arms outstretched in a gesture of dramatic ambiguity. Was she embracing The Fallen, or bidding them rise? Was she Victory or Lamentation? The inscriptions were restrained:

Their name liveth for evermore.

Keep in mind those from this place who gave their lives
in the Great War 1914–1919.

Hinckley's War Memorial spoke generously of the honour and stupidity of the people who'd made it. Honour, because they'd wanted to do right by their sons. Stupidity, because no name liveth for evermore. The names of the heroes of Hinckley were besmirched by graffiti – 'Claire is a slag' – and the rose garden planted in their memory had become a dogs' lavatory. Hinckley War Memorial was the haunt of teenage truants, a place for them to beat up park benches and practise not using the litter-bins.

On the way to Uncle Peter's I popped into St Mary's Church, the vicar of which was clearly abreast of the latest theological issues. He had opened a café in a spare vestry and was selling Nicaraguan coffee on fair-trade terms. He showed me the drum-kit used by the Youth Club, said he wanted the church to be part of the community. He had sold St Mary's sister-church and used some of the money to build a crêche; he showed me a pristine toilet with baby-changing facilities. I told him that the War Memorial in the church had fewer names on it (368) than the one on Castle Mound (387). Both memorials started with J. Abbot, but the brass tablet in St Mary's ended with A.O. Willcox, while the town's memorial ended with H.T. Young.

It was only a stupid thing to say if you didn't care about Hinckley or the men of 'D' Company who'd died for it. Hodges was killed in a ditch by a German machine-gunner one month before the Armistice, and Maw with him. One of the Paynes had been a batman. Smith was captured on May 6th 1918, but escaped behind German lines after kicking one of his guards in the bollocks and stabbing the other with his own bayonet; he received the Military Medal for that. I knew Sergeant Jaques because I had visited his grave at Packhorse Farm. Sergeant Growdridge was killed when a trench mortar landed on the battalion cookhouse, January 11th 1918 . . .

It should have occurred to me sooner: Uncle Peter was as close to Walter as I was ever going to get. The laws of genetics decree that if the father supports Leicester City, smokes Park Drive cigarettes and drinks Mild rather than Bitter, so will his son. Walter had been a stocky, round chap; so was Uncle Peter. Walter had worked all his life in the boot and shoe trade; so had Uncle Peter. Walter fought at Ypres against the Germans; so had Uncle Peter. So when Uncle Peter scoffed at the church, it was presumably because Walter had done likewise. Why, therefore, had he put himself down as Church of England on his medical records? I had always understood that the Butterworths were Methodists.

'The way he told it were like this,' said Uncle Peter. 'When he were filling in his forms, it so happened as there were a band marching past the window outside. And when the Sergeant-Major says to our Walter, "Which religion are yer?", your grandad says, "Same as that lot with the band – if it's good enough for them, it's good enough for me." And that were that. 'Cos if there were anything going for free, your grandad had to have some of it. So C–of–E he was.'

'Did he ever go to St Mary's?'

'St Mary's!?' said Uncle Peter. 'Of course he went to St Mary's. They had the best football team in Hinckley. He used to turn out for them regular. I've got a picture of him somewhere . . .'

Uncle Peter went over to a cupboard and rummaged inside.

'. . . If there were anything going for free, your grandad had to have some. Why do you think he joined up in the first place? Because if you was in the Terries you got two weeks free holiday every year. You went camping every summer. Left the missus at home and went up Skegness with yer mates. That's where he were when the War started . . . where is the bloody thing? . . . you did a bit of marching and you played a bit of cricket and you learned to shoot yer gun – this'll be it – and it were a lark. Lad like Walter, working in a factory, he weren't going to get holiday any other road. He got more than he bargained for – look at 'em, which one's yer grandad?'

It was a postcard of a football team, 19 Edwardian lads with unsmiling faces and sternly folded arms, not a Rupert Brooke among them. Their strip was: collar-less dark shirt with a bold cross on the left breast; knee-length white shorts; black socks. 'Hinckley Church United F.C. Champions SS League. Winners County Medals.'

Uncle Peter pointed to the lad with the most hair. 'That's yer man.'

Walter Butterworth grew up and fought the German Army to a standstill. He fathered six children and bought his own house. The best day of his life was March 26th 1949.

'He were so chuffed when City got to the semis,' said Uncle Peter, 'he painted his hat. He did! He had this bowler hat he used to wear, and when Leicester City got to the semi-finals in 1949 he painted it blue and white!'

The match – against Portsmouth – was played in London, at Highbury.

'I can't remember why we had to play them at the Arsenal, but any road we all went down on the train, and I'm glad we did because it were the best game of football you've ever seen. Pompey were top of the First Division then, we were bottom of the Second. No one gave us a chance. Pompey in them days were something else, invincible. Well, we chased 'em all over the park. They didn't know what hit 'em. Don Revie scored twice. Bloody belters they were. Your grandad went potty. Three-one. We couldn't believe it. "Best day of my life," he says afterwards. "Best day of my life." I believe it were, too. Didn't do us much good though. We lost at Wembley to Wolves.'

The late forties and early fifties were the glory days for Leicester City and Walter Butterworth. Home gates of 30,000 at Filbert Street, and the mortgage nearly paid off on the house in Factory Road. The Butterworths had moved there in 1935 when my mother was born. Walter was the foreman laster at one of Bennett's shoe factories in Barwell, the next village to Hinckley.

'Every Saturday dinner time when we was kids,' said Uncle Peter, 'he'd come home from work and give Clara his wages and say, "There y're, Mam." And she'd put his bus money up on the mantelpiece and keep the rest. If he wanted a pint he had to walk to work. He did! He used to walk to work in Barwell, four mile there and four mile back, to save fourpence, which were the price of a pint of Mild. One day – I can still see it now – he gets his pint pot out from under the sink and he says to me, "Our Pete, go up the road for us and get us a pint in." So off I ran up the road to Jenny's – that were the off-licence – and bugger me if I didn't fall over and drop it! Smash, all over the road. I were frit then, 'cos I knewed I were for it. I ran bawlin' all the way back – we were living in Dares Walk at the time – and as soon as he sees me he knewed as summat were up. He says, "Our Pete, what you done?" So I says, "I dropped your pot, Dad." And quick as a flash he grabbed me by the collar and he pinned me agen the kitchen wall. My feet were off the ground. And he says – giving me a shake, like – "Did you drop it afore you got to the shop or after?" Well, it were afore, weren't it, so I were saved. So he lets me down and fetches out another pot and sends me off again. And it were all right. But he would have belted me if I'd have lost his pint. Eight miles he'd walked for it, and he'd earned it. That's how it were in them days.'

My mother, Shirley Butterworth, married out of Hinckley. She wed a Barwell lad called Bernard Moore, who did his National Service in the Navy and then went into the Civil Service. My parents were living in Brazil Street, Leicester, when I was born, next door to Filbert Street. Then they moved to South Wigston, where my elder sister was born. Then my father was posted to the British Army of the Rhine. From Germany we went to Wales, from Wales to Singapore, from Singapore to Scotland. I supported Leicester City – it was in my genes – but Leicester was never home. We visited Hinckley and Barwell for Christmas, but rarely. I grew up not knowing my uncles and aunts. I still don't know the names of all my cousins, or where they live, or which of them have children.

'What is it you actually do with this journalism of yours?' asked Uncle Peter.

It didn't seem quite right that a grown man could make an honest living without having something useful to show for it, like a pair of boots. Although he'd been retired for more than ten years, Uncle Peter still bore the stigmata of his trade – calluses the size of hazel-nuts where, decade by decade, the Consol had pummelled his hands.

'The Consol?' said Uncle Peter later. 'A damned good machine. It were like this ways—'

He stopped in the middle of the pavement – we were on our way to the pub – and he crouched with his pelvis forward as if he were about to do an Elvis Presley impersonation. He mimed a Consol machine hammering tacks into a shoe.

'If you went into the room and all the Consol men were going at once,' said Uncle Peter, 'it looked like seven dogs having a jump at the same time.'

We were heading for the Queen's Head, Walter's old pub.

'See that—' Uncle Peter was pointing at nothing in particular on the other side of the road. 'I used to stand there when I were a lad and ask the folk coming out if they had any cigarette cards. I used to collect football players like no one's business.'

Uncle Peter was pointing at two cast-iron bollards set into the cornerstones of an arch, except the arch was missing. I looked again and recognised the very foundations of a factory, recently demolished. When I took a step back, I saw that it had been a considerable building. There was nothing between the Queen's Head to my right and the nude side wall of another empty factory about eighty yards down the street. I stared up into a slab of night sky.

'When I were a lad,' said Uncle Peter, 'there used to be three hundred people worked in here.'

The demolition men had boarded up part of the site and spread some barbed wire. In letters three foot high someone had daubed a desperate epitaph: 'THIS WAS HINCKLEY.'

The Queen's Head was a working-man's boozer. It was the kind of place the working-man might nip into for a swift pint on his way to the match, or after a late shift. He might take his dog there but not his best woman, unless she had a specific preference for pub grub. The atmosphere was blue with fumes from the chip frier.

'That were your grandad's place,' said Uncle Peter. 'Over there in that corner. Used to be the Snug when I were a lad.'

One wall of the old Snug had been removed to make room for a pool table, around which a posse of Hinckley bikers and their gals were tucking into scampi in baskets. The men had their hair tied up in pony-tails and wore earrings; the gals swigged Mexican beer from the bottle and belched if they felt like it. I bought Uncle Peter his pint of Mild and went over to where Walter had supped with his mates, year after year, recalling his narrow escapes in No Man's Land. He would have talked about the trenches for sure, long before anyone in Hinckley had ever tasted a scampi. I placed my hand reverently on the wood panelling where Walter must − by the law of averages − have rested the back of his Brylcreemed head.

I lifted a corner of the curtain for a peek at Walter's view of the street outside. The slate roof of the Hinckley and Barwell Co-Operative Society Model Steam Bakery (1906) still loomed above the workshop on the corner with the clock-face over the door. Nothing had changed in fifty years, except that the Hinckley and Barwell Co-Operative Society was defunct and the corner workshop had been taken over by an undertaker: 'G. Seller & Co., the family-owned funeral directors'. A Texan on the juke-box told me that everybody was somebody's plaything. One of the pool players backed into me with his bum and gave me an accidentally-on-purpose look over his shoulder, which made the gals giggle.

It struck me again, as I loitered outside No. 47, Dares Walk, that my quest for Walter's War might have been better conceived as fiction after all. The bare facts of Hinckley were too cussedly mundane for the kind of warm prose I had envisaged when I began my Great War book. I wanted to locate Walter, evoke him, retrieve his experience, make it my own. Whenever I seemed to be getting close, he slipped away.

Walter and Clara Butterworth moved to Dares Walk, a terrace of artisans' cottages, when King Street became too small for their growing family. In 1924, extra space meant two rooms upstairs, two rooms downstairs, a scullery at the back and a lavatory in the yard. Dares Walk's current occupants had all tried to individualise their front doors with those personal touches – coach-lamps, storm porches, hanging baskets – so irritating to students of vernacular architecture. The new jemmy-proof double glazing of No. 47 advertised that it had been recently burgled. A yellow sticker supplied by Leicestershire Constabulary warned that all callers would be asked to provide proof of identity.

Even with my nose pressed up against the past, it stayed jemmy-proof. Uncle Peter had told me that, to make an extra few coppers, Walter had repaired shoes in his spare time. The kitchen table at Dares Walk had been a cobbler's bench, covered over with a board at mealtimes. If there was ever any tinned salmon in the house, Walter used to keep the tins for holding his tacks. I wanted to confirm this secret knowledge. I wanted to knock on the door of No. 47, Dares Walk, and ask permission to inspect the kitchen cupboards for salmon tins.

The sense of Hinckley for which I yearned remained stubbornly out of reach. Old photographs of its streets conveyed that sunny Edwardian combination of the industrial with the agricultural which disappeared in the deluge of the Great War. Never such innocence again. No electricity, no universal suffrage. Horses in the streets, not cars. And butcher's boys with wicker baskets. Despite the increasing number of factories and workshops, the Hinckley of Walter's youth had still been a recognisably Anglo-Saxon settlement. The ancient tracks and pathways of Saxon times were still traceable in the winding 'jitties' – like Dares Walk – which provided short cuts from one part of Hinckley to another. The open space where Station Road and Castle Street intersected, known as the Borough, was still the same gossip exchange it had been for nearly a thousand years of English history.

I wandered Hinckley's jitties in a Walter-induced trance. It felt satisfying to follow his footsteps, to open the same doors, to brush against the same walls, to drink pints of Mild, but it was an expression of personal need rather than research. Important factual questions remained unasked. I didn't feel able to ask Walter's children how long he'd been married to Clara when Walter Noël Gordon was born. Other questions were unanswerable. Men returning from the trenches were ravenous for a taste of life; what had Walter wanted most – toast, steak and kidney pie, fresh milk? What had Walter said when he crossed the threshold of 3 King Street to announce his unexpected return from the trenches? What had Clara been doing at that moment? How had it been when Walter held his son for the first time? What souvenirs did he bring back?

Soldiers on leave often found themselves alienated from the civilian life of Blighty. By passing through the fire of battle they were marked out for ever from those who had stayed at home. The War changed everything that mattered. Once they had got over their joyful reunion, what would Walter and Clara have talked about? They had nothing in common. He'd been living like a hunted animal for the past year. The man who came home to Clara was stronger, coarser, louder, more dangerous than the one who'd marched away.

And what of Clara? Had she got a job, new friends? Had her life been quite interesting since Walter had gone away? Had she farmed out Walter Noël Gordon to a wet-nurse while earning good money in the factories? Or had she become embittered, coping alone with the new-born, ekeing out a frugal existence on her niggardly separation allowance? There must have been awkward moments – misunderstandings, arguments, sudden rages, amorous makings-up. A week or ten days was too short a time to get to know each other all over again. How could she understand the War? How could Walter explain the slaughter at the Hohenzollern Redoubt or the bungling at Gommecourt? Men on leave tended to keep quiet where the sensibilities of womenfolk were concerned. They didn't talk about the utter indecency of death in battle, how shellfire and machine-gun bullets annihilated the manliness of men and scattered it in the mud, how the chemistry of death turned men black, how all the dead were trampled by the living and gnawed by rats. The Great War was too much for Clara's kitchen. Walter would have shut up about it, or muttered gruffly, or shrugged it off. Or would he have blurted it all out and horrified her with one-tenth of the truth?

In fiction I could have answered these questions, taken a confident narrative line. I could have painted that scene as Walter and Clara stepped into the chill grey dawn for his last walk down Station Road. They would have gone in silence apart from the clink-chink of Walter's bayonet on his belt and the crunch of his boots on the cobbles – him weighed down with his kit, her with the thought that she might never see him again. On the platform of Hinckley station, as the Leicester train clanked to a halt, they would have hidden their last clinging kisses among the slamming of doors and hissing of steam. And then, for her sake, Walter would have forced a smile, cracked a joke and slung his kit aboard. I can see Clara as the train pulls away, keeping pace with Walter's carriage until the platform runs out – whereat, in a gesture of hope and pride, she lifts up Walter Noël Gordon, swaddled in her second-best shawl, and holds him aloft like the

Madonna of Albert, Our Lady of Brebières, until the red light of the guard's van finally winks out, leaving her alone again to fret and pray another year, or until the Great War claims her man for ever.

7

LENS

And I saw white bones in the cinder shard,
Bones without number.
Many the muscled bodies charred,
And few remember.

Wilfred Owen, 'Miners'

The Fifth Leicesters to whom Walter returned after his leave were unrecognisable as the battalion he'd joined two years before. Three-quarters of them were dead or permanently maimed. Those who'd been salvaged and sent back, like Walter, wore the weary air of hardened gamblers. Life and death in the trenches were governed by battalion orders and the chance distribution of enemy ordnance. Anything beyond the radius of a man's platoon was irrelevant. The imperatives which had launched Britain into War – Justice, Honour – had withered during the Battle of the Somme to a single imponderable: Survival.

By the time the Somme offensive was closed down at the end of 1916, the enthusiastic volunteers of Britain's New Armies had come to realise that they were in a fight to the death. As the better British generals set themselves to learn from their mistakes, the men faced up to a prolonged campaign of endurance. The new drafts arriving in France became, in Sassoon's memorable phrase, droves of victims. No matter how many Germans the British killed there were always more to take their place, and vice-versa. Every gap which one side managed to make in the enemy ranks was promptly plugged by new hordes. The Great War would continue until, on one side or the other, the supply of young men ran out. That's when the generals would find their room to manoeuvre; that's when the cavalry would pour in; that's when, at long last, the real fighting could begin.

The more pessimistic resigned themselves to a war of seven or ten or even 20 years. Industrialisation had given the machinery of destruction a momentum so powerful that it was now feasible for the Great War to go on for ever. By a curious symmetry, the adoption of steel helmets on both sides of No Man's Land was recognised as a defining moment. 'The dethronement of the soft cap,' says Blunden, 'clearly symbolized the change that was coming over the war, the induration from a personal crusade into a vast machine of violence.' Ernst Junger, author of the German classic *Storm of Steel*, says the Somme was where chivalry disappeared for ever: 'Like all noble and personal feelings it had to give way to the new tempo of battle and to the rule of the machine. Here the new Europe revealed itself for the first time in combat.'

The passage from innocence to experience was further symbolised for the Fifth Leicesters by the loss of Lieutenant-Colonel Jones in April 1917. Excepting a few weeks in 1915, when he'd been slightly wounded by a shell splinter at Wulverghcm, Jones had led the Fifth Leicesters since their mobilisation. According to Hills:

There was not an officer or a man who did not regret his

going. There never was a trench post which he did not visit, no matter how exposed or how dangerous the approach to it. Moreover, he was never downhearted, and while he was in it, the Battalion Headquarters of the 5th Leicestershire Regiment was known thoroughout the Division as one of the most cheerful, if not the most cheerful, spot in France.

As a proven leader, Jones was an asset to the British Army. The length of his leave was calculated to allow the refreshment of those qualities essential to further usefulness. But a democratic instinct begrudges him twelve times the allowance that Walter had earned in similar circumstances. Walter had been with the battalion since the beginning; he too had been wounded; he too had visited exposed and dangerous trench posts; he too had been cheerful, maybe. Walter had earned ten days' leave, maximum; Lieutenant-Colonel Jones received three months, and never came back. After his leave he was transferred to another battalion and disappears from Hills' narrative.

The Fifth Leicesters' new commander was an erstwhile Major from the East Yorkshire Regiment, J.B.O. Trimble M.C. That's all. J-for-John? J-for-James? Jeremy? Jasper? We don't know, are not told. Tall man? Pipe-smoker? Hills doesn't say. Perhaps he was resentful at the promotion going to an outsider. There was no shortage of Majors within the 46th Division who would have felt entitled to command the Fifth Leicesters. But by this stage, expediency had reduced the sensitivity of GHQ and the War Office towards such proprietorial feelings, especially among the Territorials. The Regulars driving the British war machine had taken the doctrines of attrition to heart. Raw manpower would count for most in the battles of 1917. Victory would go to the side most ruthless in using its numbers to wear down the enemy. Ambitious, hard-bitten Regulars – 'thrusters' or 'fire-eaters' in the parlance of the time – were more likely to be efficient in this respect than the 'temporary gentlemen' or 'civilians in uniform' who swelled the officer cadres of the Territorial Divisions and the New Armies.

In the French and German Armies, where divisions and regiments were categorised by number, the local attachments of individual men were subsumed in the cause of national survival. France had been invaded and defiled; every Frenchman felt the obligation to fight, regardless of where he had been born. The British, at least at the beginning, felt no such blinding motivation; they were fighting on foreign soil to uphold an abstraction. But whereas an abstraction – Honour, Justice – can lure a young man to enlist, it is less likely on its own to inspire him to charge with his bayonet, especially when he has seen at first hand the various effects that shellfire and gunshot can inflict on the human body. Men in the trenches needed rum or something stronger to get them over the top. Time and time again the veterans of the Great War attested that comradeship, esprit de corps, brotherly love, was the thing that pulled them through. And the basis of comradeship was regimental pride. Men recruited and trained for the Irish Rangers or the Highland Light Infantry most definitely did not want to end up scrapping for their lives alongside Cheshires or Somersets. The Fifth Leicesters did not want to be led by an East Yorks, but the Army made sure that that is what they got.

On the day when J.B.O. Trimble formally took command – April 23rd 1917 – the Fifth Leicesters marched south from Béthune for a couple of days as Brigade Reserve at the Double Crassier slag-heap. The Canadians, who had cleared Vimy Ridge in their spectacular assault of April 9th, were now harrying the German withdrawal towards Lens and the Leicesters believed that the capture of the town was the next objective. Given the haste of the German withdrawal and the undoubted prowess of the

Canadians in pursuit, it was hoped that Lens might fall quite easily. In fact, under their new and untested Colonel, the Leicesters were heading for some of the most savage fighting of the War. 'Our new sector,' says Hills, 'was one of the worst we ever held.'

One year to the week after our first visit to Beuvry, we were back. After months of haggling, my wife had finally agreed to return to the battlefields one more time, the very last. After this, I had agreed, there would be no more trenches, no more war cemeteries. If I didn't find Walter this time, *tant pis*. It wasn't fair on the children. After this, it was holidays in Scotland for ever.

Nothing had changed at Beuvry's municipal camp-site. Under *le patron*'s policy of apartheid, campers were still segregated according to nationality. We pitched camp in the English kraal, shaded by the same sycamore tree that had sheltered us the year before. Gabriel unpacked his football and kicked it straight into our neighbour's soup. The subsequent conversation, though brief, established that they were childless, hungry, and moving on in the morning . . . which was a relief to us all.

After the traditional Beuvry supper of sausages, baked beans and coal grit, we motored into Béthune for a taste of old times. Like Ypres, Béthune had been ruined by the War and carefully restored; the steep medieval gables around the Grand Place displayed no date earlier than 1920. One of these narrow buildings had been the Globe, where Graves and Blunden and the Prince of Wales had played billiards and sipped grenadine to while away their off-duty moments. There were no clues, no plaques, no bronze inscriptions to signify that during the Battle of Loos the Grand Place had been the Piccadilly Circus of the Western Front. In the Hôtel de France or the Lion d'Or soldiers met friends whom they hadn't seen for 20 years. Every bar was crowded, every table taken. There was a two-hour wait for a seat in the shack that an enterprising barber had set up at the base of the great belfry in the middle of the square. There were cake-shops and *salons de thé*. There was a theatre. There were off-duty nurses. There were brothels for men and separate ones for officers.

We joined the Béthunois at their evening promenade. They kissed each other four times in greeting, shook hands all round, trailed fragrant vapours through the day's last mellow sunbeams. Robert Graves had hated them:

> They suck enormous quantities of money out of us . . .
> The prices are ridiculous and the stuff bad. In the brewery
> at Béthune, the other day, I saw barrels of already thin
> beer being watered from the canal with a hose pipe. The
> *estaminet*-keepers water it further . . .

We took an outside table and ate ice cream. The Union Jack billowed from the façade of the *Mairie*, along with the flags of all the other nations of the European Union. Of all the cars parked in the Grand Place, the only rusty ones were British. And when the bill came I realised how little one pound was worth.

The Leicesters thought their immediate objective was the city of Lens. Lying at the heart of France's richest coalfield, it was a prize the Germans were determined to hold. Despite the War, the collieries on either side of No Man's Land had been kept working round the clock. Each pit complex was known as a Cité, comprising its workshops, slag-heaps and rows of miners' cottages. A score of these self-contained Cités had sprouted like a fungus on the plain north and east of Vimy Ridge, connected by a network of roads, railways and canals which had all been smashed to pieces. 'The best description of Lens,' says Milne, 'is that it was perfectly bloody. From the time the battalion arrived to the time they left they always hated the place.'

The German trenches in Lens ran from cellar to cellar in a complicated gestalt of overlapping zig-zags. The shattered streets of the Cités, which were under constant surveillance from dozens of slag-heaps, were almost impossible for any attacking force to read tactically, even with the benefit of aerial reconnaisance. The Germans knew every nook and cranny, the Leicesters hardly knew where to start. Street-fighting had never formed part of their training; they could never be sure who was in the next trench or the next house:

> The whole place was chaos [says Milne]. It was a rabbit warren infested by wild men . . . Never was there such a reign of battle, murder and sudden death . . . Savages rushed at each other with cold steel . . . Friend and foe were mixed in a welter of slag, bricks and blood.

The Fifth Leicesters' first tour sent them into an exposed salient called Cooper Trench in front of Cité St Pierre. It was overlooked from every direction and declared unapproachable during daylight. In addition to field artillery and machine guns, the Germans used their trench mortars to deadly effect. Having occupied the very positions they were now bombing, they knew the range of every target. Hills describes watching a mortar methodically working along a street, dropping a 240lb bomb on each house before moving on to the next: 'It was a nerve-racking performance for those who lived in the cellars and had to watch the shells coming nearer, knowing that to go into the street meant instant death at the hands of some sniper.'

I had marked Cooper Trench in green ink on my map, but as soon as we got to Lens I abandoned all hope of finding it.

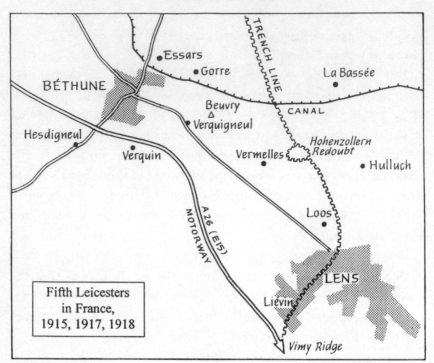

The city had sprawled so far beyond its 1917 boundaries as to be unrecognisable. Béthune, Gommecourt, Fonquevillers, Ypres – these places had grown since the War in a recognisably organic way. Lens was manic by comparison, dense with traffic, people, shops, signs, flashing lights, flyovers, multi-lane intersections. Lens was bad news to anyone trying to navigate by trench map. All I knew about Cooper Trench was that it was near Cité St Pierre, but I couldn't see any signs pointing to Cité St Pierre. All the old coal-mines had been shut down and demolished. I saw a sign pointing to Lievin.

'Go,' I said.

'Where?' she asked.

'Lievin. Lievin.'

'What about your trench?'

'The trench is gone, forget it. Lievin. Lievin.'

Cooper Trench had gone, but there was a place in the suburb of Lievin where I knew Walter had been. It was near a bridge, near a river. Coal-mines could be demolished and railways uprooted. Dugouts and trenches could be filled in and built over. Rivers were timeless. The bridge over the River Souchez at Red Mill in Lievin, that's where I would find Walter.

Lens was the objective of the 46th Division, but it was not intended to be captured. On May 25th 1917, after a big parade at which Major-General Thwaites handed out medals, he informed the officers of the Fifth Leicesters that their task, in conjunction with the Canadian 3rd and 4th Divisions, was to take part in a series of feints to distract the Germans while Sir Douglas Haig prepared for the Big Push of 1917 – the battle at Ypres that would become notorious as Passchendaele. Haig had ordered that the feints at Lens should involve deliberate preparation of attack, concentration of artillery and economy of infantry. He told his commanders to focus on the two heights commanding the approaches to Lens – Hill 70 to the north and Hill 65 in the south-western suburb of Lievin. The British and Canadians would fight their way forward, Cité by Cité, until these positions had been secured.

As part of this strategy, the Fifth Leicesters were assigned the capture of Fosse 3, a slag-heap which had been heavily fortified by the Germans as a defensive buttress to Hill 65 itself. A plan of the German defences was marked out with flags in the fields around Marqueffles Farm in the back areas near Vimy Ridge. Every day 'B' and 'C' Companies rehearsed their attack until each man knew exactly what was expected of him. Divisional Staff came along to make sure that proper emphasis was placed on 'mopping-up' after the initial charge – a tactic that was considered novel enough, even in 1917, to require inverted commas when written down. Afterwards, everybody who had seen the practice felt assured that the attack on Fosse 3 would be a great success.

The Fifth Leicesters left Marqueffles and moved into Lievin's ghostly ruins on June 6th 1917. For the first time, the officers were dressed the same as the men – to make them less conspicuous to German snipers. The Leicesters occupied trenches at the foot of Riaumont Hill in the centre of Lievin and made their final preparations for their night assault. Maps were issued, weapons and stores were checked, patrols crawled out to make sure the wire was cut. At 2030 hours on June 8th the British artillery barrage opened and the first salvo scored a direct hit on a German ammunition dump, illuminating the whole of the subsequent fight with a fierce red blaze.

'C' Company under Captain Moore went into action first. They swarmed up the Fosse 3 slag-heap and threw themselves at the two German-held trenches at the summit, Boot Trench and Brick Trench. Sergeant Needham single-handedly accounted for the crew of a trench-mortar emplacement. Second-Lieutenant Banwell ran amok. Armed like his men with rifle and bayonet, Banwell slashed and lunged at every German in sight, killing eight. One who tried to escape was chased to the edge of the slag-heap and kicked into the lake below, where he broke his neck and died. According to Hills, by the time Boot and Brick Trenches were in British hands, at least 80 Germans had been killed . . . according to Hills.

'B' Company, meanwhile, had attacked on the left. Their immediate objective was a strongly fortified position known as 'the L-shaped building'. Their commander, Captain Wynne, had decided to stay with his men despite being virtually worn out with fever. He led them straight into a hail of machine-gun bullets and died instantly. His two junior officers were also wounded, 'B'

Company was flattened. As night fell, they tried to dig in a few yards forward of their start line.

The failure of 'B' Company had left the men on Fosse 3 dangerously exposed. They were open to enfilade fire from the summit of Hill 65, as well as from a nearby strongpoint in the ruins of an electricity-generating plant. The darkness that had helped 'C' Company's attack now impeded their plans for defence because they were unable to observe what was going on in the ground to the east. Here, the slag-heap sloped down steeply to the banks of the River Souchez, which had been blocked by so much battle débris that it had overflowed and formed a wide, shallow lake. This blind spot formed an obvious place for the assembly of any counter-attack. Nevertheless, the Leicesters consolidated what they had won by 'reversing' the parapets of their newly captured trenches, as they had practised in training. They were judged to be well-established by the time Brigade HQ got Staff officers forward to check their position.

Just before dawn, the Germans counter-attacked in strength. 'C' Company's sentries reported large numbers of men closing on them from three sides. Captain Moore, wishing to conserve his last remaining supplies of ammunition, told his men to hold their fire and break out the Mills bombs. As the leading Germans came within range the first volley of grenades was thrown. Nothing happened . . . they were duds. Unbelievably, the Leicesters had been sent into action with Mills bombs without detonators. Again 'C' Company retired in haste, first to the edge of the slag-heap and then to the rows of miners' cottages at the bottom. Their night in Boot and Brick Trenches had cost them one dead, 28 wounded and two captured:

At the time [says Hills] the withdrawal from the slagheap seemed like a defeat, but had we stayed our casualties would have been far worse and the result the same; for with daylight nothing could have lived on the heap so long as the Generating Station and Hill 65 remained in German hands.

Major-General Thwaites was free with his congratulations when he next visited the Leicesters, but repeated that the original objective remained: Fosse 3 was vital to the capture of Hill 65, which was vital to the wider aim of encircling Lens. Indeed, the need to preoccupy the town's German defenders had become more pressing than ever now that the first stage of Haig's offensive at Ypres had got under way at Messines. It was deemed crucial to the success of the Flanders operation to hold German reserves in the south. The Lincolns were sent in to complete the capture of the slag-heap at Fosse 3, while the Canadians made progress on the other side of the River Souchez, seizing the electricity-generating station. If the Leicesters could complete the capture of the Fosse 3 workings, the way would be clear for Thwaites to make a concerted effort on Hill 65 – preferably before the Canadians could get there.

As night fell on June 21st 1917, the Fifth Leicesters – installed in Brick and Boot Trenches – received warning that a gas barrage was going to be laid on the positions below which were still partially occupied by Germans. The barrage would be launched from the Canadian side of the Souchez, using the recently developed Livens gas projectors. This new-fangled weapon consisted of tubes which could hurl canisters of liquid gas up to a mile away. It wasn't a terribly powerful delivery system but it did have one great advantage: hundreds of canisters could be fired at once, bringing an element of surprise to the use of gas. Hitherto, the first sight of a gas cloud had given the Germans warning to put on their respirators. With the Livens projectors, the gas would be among them before they knew what had hit them. The system had been tested by the Canadians a couple of weeks before and had been judged suitable to the close-built confines of an urban battle zone.

At Zero, the Fifth Leicesters' sentries heard the dull 'whump' of the Livens canisters being launched and waited with interest for this latest novelty of the War to do its work. Within seconds they were drenched with fumes as 600 canisters spewing phosgene landed on them. The Canadians had fired at the wrong target. Instead of hitting the Germans in the mine workings below, they had gassed their British comrades on top of the slag-heap. The Leicesters groped through the fumes to rouse their companions. But the attack was so sudden and intense that all they managed was a few gargled words before they collapsed – clutching their throats, floundering like men in fire or lime. Phosgene was more powerful than chlorine but affected the body in the same way, liquefying the tissues of the lungs so that men choked on their own corrupted froth. Casualties were still being brought out at dawn, eyes writhing in their hanging faces. With the exception of Captain Moore, who had been rewarded with a spell of leave for his role in the earlier fight, the whole of 'C' Company had been blotted from the battalion roll.

Cost to the Fifth Leicesters of Livens projector demonstration: 24 men killed, 62 wounded. Cost to German defenders of Fosse 3: sore ribs from savage laughter.

The Fifth Leicesters first went in to rest at Red Mill between May 12th and May 15th 1917. From then on, whenever they were in brigade support, they were regular visitors. Red Mill wasn't a mill, it was a brick château occupying wooded grounds in the suburb of Rollencourt between a crossroads and a bridge over the Souchez River. According to Hills:

The weather was bright and warm, so a dam was built, and we soon had an excellent bathing pool, much patronized by all ranks. 2nd Lieut J.C. Barrett was the star performer, and never left the water, so that those who had nothing better to do used to 'go and see the Signalling Officer swim' – it was one of the recognised recreations of the place.

As a map reference, Red Mill should have been unmissable. All I had to do was find the River Souchez and follow it. Unfortunately, there was no river; the Souchez had dried up. All of Lieven's coal-mines had been eradicated except for a few slag-heaps which had been planted with shrubs and trees like miniature Alps. The only obvious landmark remaining was Riaumont Hill, and it was by taking my bearings on this that I eventually came to Rollencourt crossroads. A narrow road then led me to the bridge I had been seeking.

The grounds of Red Mill had become Lievin's athletics stadium, and the foundations of the old mansion house were occupied by changing rooms named in honour of one Michel Gallet. The River Souchez had been reduced to a canalised stream; what was marked on my trench map as a bridge was now a culvert. This was where Walter had come to watch the Signalling Officer swim . . .

In front of me was a street plan of Lievin with its civic amenities picked out in glowing colours. The Souchez was marked as a thin blue flourish in the green wedge of the Parc de Rollencourt; upstream it disappeared into another culvert under the Rue Rabelais. A circle had been drawn around the exact square metre on the map where I was standing: '*Vous êtes ici.*' Except that I wasn't '*ici*' or even close. I was inside a trench map of 1917, feeling confused.

In the aftermath of the Livens gas disaster, the Fifth Leicesters were reduced to three companies of three platoons each. General Thwaites blamed the Canadians for what had happened; their sappers 'hadn't been informed' that the Fosse 3 slag-heap was occupied. Yet with Hill 65 now within his grasp, General Thwaites was determined to show the Canadians and Sir Douglas Haig that he could take it. A big British feint had been scheduled for the end of June, and as part of this General Thwaites declared that the 138th Brigade would finally capture Hill 65. Three battalions would attack in waves. The severely depleted Fifth Leicesters would be on the right, the Fourth Leicesters would be in the centre and the Fifth Staffords on the left. Once again, the assault would be practised on a course marked out with flags. Once again, particular attention would be paid to mopping-up. Once again, when the time came, the Fifth Leicesters trudged up from Red Mill to do or die.

The attacking battalions filed into the Line on the evening of June 27th 1917. The guides didn't know where they were going. Everyone got lost. The Canadians on the right launched a dummy attack without warning, which brought down a fierce retaliatory barrage from the Germans. By 0500 hours, the Leicesters were in place. They checked their stores, tested their communication lines and tried to rest. The weather was dull and close, threatening thunder. The Germans, suspecting that an attack was imminent, had sent up observation balloons as well as spotter planes. As the Leicesters readied themselves to go over the top, it seemed certain that they must be seen. Then, as Zero 1910 hours approached, the storm broke.

The British barrage opened on a 14-mile front to give the impression that a large-scale offensive for Lens was under way. Simultaneously, thunder and lightning tore the black clouds apart, multiplying the deafening effect of the bombardment. For once the weather was on the side of the British; the downpour temporarily blinded the Germans and allowed the Leicesters to crawl from their trenches unobserved. As the barrage lengthened, they stood up and advanced over the slopes of Hill 65 in perfect formation. The leading Leicesters saw with relief that the artillery had done its work. 'A' and 'B' Companies reached their objectives, Adjunct and Adjacent Trenches, without opposition. Despite their hours of practising, there was no one left for Walter and the rest of 'D' Company to mop up. The Germans had been caught off balance by the storm and had retreated.

At 1940 hours, by which time the heaviest rain had passed over, a runner arrived at Battalion HQ to report that the battle had been a complete success. The Fifth Leicesters consolidated behind a defensive barrage and, in the absence of anyone to bayonet, contented themselves with hunting for souvenirs. Hills snaffled a telephone. The fight for Hill 65 had cost them another three officers and 90 men wounded, mostly in the retaliatory shelling which followed the initial assault.

In the standard histories of the Great War, the Leicesters' battle for Lens rates hardly a mention. The Canadian contribution is usually noted in passing, but rarely that of the 46th Division. Yet in the last battle for Hill 65 the division lost in the order of 50 officers and 1,000 men killed, wounded or captured. Haig, in his despatches, noted that all his objectives at Lens had been gained, along with '300 prisoners and a number of machine guns'.

General Thwaites was well pleased. On July 8th 1917, five days after the Leicesters had been withdrawn to rest, he attended a church parade to distribute medals. He told the Leicesters and Lincolns that he was proud to command them. Milne records the scene:

Praise had belched from the lips which had often fulminated censure . . . The men were happy. The ranks were thin but that did not bother them. They did not think of the ragged bundles of flesh and clothing lying about the ruins of Lens . . .

They knew that private soldiers are not paid to think but to do as they are told . . . So they marched off parade as gaily as their heavy ammunition boots would allow. Then they filled their stomachs with ample rations of meat and fresh vegetables, and in the afternoon delighted their souls with the one thing that really matters to the British nation – football.

8

THE RAID

To these I turn, in these I trust—
Brother Lead and Sister Steel.
        Siegfried Sassoon, 'The Kiss'

The Fifth Leicesters' first hard-core, battalion-strength trench raid came comparatively late in their career. It was conceived by General Thwaites as a formal declaration of intent on arrival at his new sector of operations following the 46th Division's withdrawal from Lens. On July 20th 1917, after three weeks in safe billets with good food and plenty of sport, the Leicesters were sent into the Line opposite the German-held village of Hulluch, just a few hundred yards south of where they had failed so terribly at the Hohenzollern two years before. After six days' familiarisation with the trench system, the Leicesters were pulled out to begin practising their raid in earnest.

Conforming to the prevailing orthodoxy of GHQ, Major-General Thwaites regarded raids as essential not only for achieving specific objectives, such as gathering intelligence from prisoners, but as an all-purpose tonic against the inertia of trench life. Raids were deemed excellent for training because they sharpened tactical awareness at Company level and exposed junior officers to the responsibilities of leadership in hazardous situations. Raids exerted supremacy over No Man's Land, thereby preventing the Germans from ever relaxing completely. And, in so far as they were meant to inflict greater damage on the Germans than they cost the British, raids contributed useful increments to the constant battle of attrition. As a result of Thwaites' enthusiasm, says the Official History of the 46th Division, many clever coups were effected:

> This system of training improved the fighting capacity of the Division to such an extent that former reverses were forgotten, or remembered only in the determination to wipe them out by achieving decisive success in the future.

This official view of raids was ridiculed by the men who had to carry them out. In practical terms, raids rarely achieved their objectives and always cost casualties. The men called them 'stunts' – little bits of theatre intended to make the various Staffs look good in their reports to each other.

The objective chosen by General Thwaites for the Fifth Leicesters' raid was a 300-yard section of the German line west of the village of Hulluch. The multiple aims were: to distract German attention from a Canadian attack on Hill 70; to destroy an extremely irritating trench mortar known as 'the Goose'; to kill Germans and inflict maximum damage on their entrenchments; to capture prisoners for purposes of identification. Divisional artillery was given two weeks to cut the thick enemy wire, in the expectation that low-key shoots over an extended period would nullify German suspicions that an attack was imminent.

Divisional Staff – comfortably ensconced in their familiar old château at Hesdigneul – marked out a model of the German trenches with flags. The attack was practised first by day, then by night. A system of lamp signals was devised to control the progress of the raiders once their attack had begun. Demolition parties were trained in how to place and prime their charges. Finally, just in case any passing spy might be in any doubt about what was intended, a large notice-board bearing the word 'Hulluch' was erected to indicate the position of the village in relation to the German trenches.

On August 14th 1917, the Fifth Leicesters collected their special stores for the raid and handed in all pay-books, badges and identity discs. At 1000 hours the following morning, they paraded for inspection and marched through Vermelles. A German shell landed in the middle of 'B' Company as it was passing Mansion House Dump, wiping out practically a whole platoon. Cost of raid before it had started: 11 NCOs and men killed; 14 wounded.

Throughout the previous two weeks of training, the Fifth Leicesters had kept a squad of men in the firing line to monitor the progress of the artillery's attempts to cut the German wire. The leader of this squad, Second-Lieutenant Brooke, was waiting in Lone Trench when the rest of the battalion arrived: there weren't enough gaps in the wire. At Colonel Trimble's request, the raid was postponed for a further 24 hours.

The Leicesters' attack was put off, but the Canadians' assault on Hill 70 was not. The Leicesters spent the next day watching the progress of the battle they had been intended to support. At one point, as the Germans massed for a counter-attack behind Hulluch, they offered an unmissable target to the Leicesters' machine-gunners and it was the 'terrific execution' effected by these teams, according to Hills, that enabled the Canadians to hold Hill 70 once it had been captured.

As night fell on August 16th 1917, the Leicesters left Lone

Trench for their assembly positions in front of Hulluch. This time the artillery had done its job and Zero was confirmed at 2258 hours. Duckboard bridges were laid across the British front trench. The men blacked each others' faces. The barrage started promptly.

Walter, in 'D' Company, under Captain Shields, was on the right. 'A' Company, under Captain Petch, was on the left. 'B' Company, under Captain Marriot, was in support. Two sections of 'C' Company provided the demolition parties. Everyone got across No Man's Land in good order and jumped into the German front-line trench, shouting his name as he landed. Two Germans were killed, but most of the trench was found to be empty apart from bundles of barbed wire.

It was a thick, black night. Captains Petch and Shields had arranged to call each other's names as they advanced, to make sure their respective companies were keeping in touch. As the two men pressed on towards the German second line, Shields' voice stopped suddenly with an awful cry. The Germans had begun pumping shells into the box marked out by the British defensive barrage, and he'd taken a direct hit. One leg had been blown away, the other was held together by shreds of integument. The rest of 'D' Company continued their advance without him and reached the German third line. As bombers formed trench blocks, the section detailed to blow up 'the Goose' set off to find it. Several Germans were found and killed, but there was a disconcerting lack of general opposition. Apart from stragglers, it seemed that the whole German garrison had managed to hide or escape. Hills, who was monitoring the progress of the raid at Battalion HQ, was able to follow the Leicesters' progress by listening to an intercept of the telephone messages between the German company commander and his own Head-quarters: 'We are being attacked . . . Front line penetrated . . .

Second line wrecked . . . Third line entered . . . Send up two sections . . .'

The German reinforcements came up separately. One section bombed its way towards the Leicesters' barricade in Hicks Alley; the other came up over the open, where they charged into a sustained burst from an 'A' Company machine gun. At this point, the signal flares fired at Battalion HQ to order the Leicesters' withdrawal failed to ignite. Runners had to be sent forward to call the raiders back. Captain Shields was carried in by his Sergeant-Major, but Captain Marriott of 'B' Company was missing, presumed killed. The 'D' Company men who had gone looking for 'the Goose' were likewise nowhere to be found. As the final stragglers were rounded up, the cost of the raid could be reckoned: 12 officers and men killed or missing; 51 officers and men wounded; 3 men believed captured. Tally of captured Germans: nil. Number of trench mortars destroyed: nil. Damage to enemy morale: nil.

Walter survived but his 'D' Company commander, Captain Shields, would never fight again. When he reached hospital the surgeons amputated his shattered leg immediately:

> It is still recorded as a unique feat [says Hills] that throughout the operation neither the patient's pulse nor temperature altered, thanks to his wonderful constitution. The other leg soon healed, and within a few months he was hopping over fences in England in the best of spirits.

General Thwaites appeared the following morning to congratulate the Leicesters on their 'efforts', but there was no disguising that the raid had been a failure. Instead of catching the enemy off guard, the Leicesters had walked into a trap. As Hills says:

There is no doubt the enemy had been prepared for us. The rapidity with which his barrage started, the partly wired trenches, empty dugouts and absence of garrison all pointed to this . . . The few [Germans] we found were those who had been too slow in getting away.

9

GORRE

In silks and satins the ladies went
Where the breezes sighed and the poplars bent,
Taking the air of a Sunday morn
Midst the red of poppies and the gold of corn . . .
Crosbie Garstin, 'Chemin des Dames'

On Sunday morning my wife took the children to that erstwhile artillery observation post, Beuvry Church, while I twiddled with the guy-ropes of our tent and stowed rations in high branches to keep the ants at bay. Afterwards we drove to Vimy Ridge, played hide-and-seek among the grassy craters and ate ice cream in No Man's Land. Lying back with the sun in my face, it was impossible to imagine anything better.

'There was an old woman at church who knew about the War,' said my wife. 'I told her you were writing a book. She said she had some old photos of English soldiers.'

Walter and the Fifth Leicesters arrived in Beuvry in December 1917, having picked up a new Commanding Officer on their way north from Hulluch. He was a South African, Lieutenant-Colonel R.W. Currin D.S.O. The Leicesters produced a Christmas card in his honour showing a German with a pained expression being kicked from the top of a slag-heap. Hills says Currin was typical of the colonial fire-eater:

> He at once terrified us with his language, which can only be described as volcanic, and won our respect by his wonderful fearlessness . . . In trenches he would wander about with his hands in his pockets, often with neither helmet or gas-bag and quite heedless of whether or not the enemy could see him. More than once he was shot at and more than once he had a narrow escape at the hands of some hostile sniper.

On Christmas Eve, the Leicesters feasted in style: roast pork; potatoes and sprouts; Christmas pud; barrels of beer. The festivities climaxed with a search of the Beuvry river for an anonymous sergeant-major who'd been reported missing in a dangerous state of inebriation. Hills says he was found safe and sound, snoring in a sentry-box with his false teeth clamped in his fist.

The Old Lady of Beuvry knew nothing about any river. There was a ditch of stagnant water behind the canal, but – *pouf!* – how could she tell? She had not been born in 1917. Her brother had been born in 1917. She showed me a photograph of him, aged six, saluting cutely in a cut-down British officer's uniform. Madame had been born in 1925. Her father had been a tailor at Sailly Labourse; he'd made uniforms for *'tous les soldats Anglais'*. I was given a photograph of a man on a handsome horse.

Madame wrote down her name in quavering italics: *Adeline Guemappe*. I borrowed her pen to make notes. She exhaled garlic halitosis and cabbage smells in my face. I liked her. She laughed at her own dotage. She showed me what she kept in her sideboard drawer – wizened envelopes and a lifetime's collection of parcel string. She burrowed deeper and brought out some glass slides, thick as tiles, five to a box, each separated by a thin membrane of tissue paper. The glass slides flickered into silvery life when I held them up to the light: moustachioed French reservists in Napoleonic collars; British Tommies with shy grins; stiff subalterns with false smiles . . .

'See!'

Madame pointed to the corner of her over-furnished room where a pier table, half-hidden under a cascade of dusty foliage, was recognisable as the main studio prop in many of the old photographs. Madame Guemappe showed me brass shell-cases which had been turned into vases, and a clock-face surrounded by brightly polished rifle cartridges. I murmured appreciatively over her collection of postcards of war-ravaged villages. I pointed to some passport photos pinned above the mantelshelf.

'*Mes frères.*'

My French was too bad to understand more than one sentence in three, but the gist of what Adeline Guemappe had to say was that she had lost everything. She gestured towards the photograph of the little boy in the British uniform: he'd been wounded and taken prisoner by the Germans in the Second World War, and had died a lunatic. Her younger brother – a strong, good-looking Gallic type with thick black hair – had been deported by the Gestapo and killed in a concentration camp on the Baltic coast. She insisted on finding an atlas so that she could point to the place: Warnemude.

'What,' I asked, 'do you feel towards the Germans?'

'*Ils me dégoutent.*'

Adeline Guemappe wanted me to understand the painful tragedy of her life. Her father had died young in a car crash;

her brothers had been tortured and killed by the Germans in the Second World War; her husband had succumbed to an early heart attack; her only son lived in the South and didn't visit as often as he should. She hardly saw her grandchildren from one year to the next. Behind Adeline I sensed the vast European sorority for whom she spoke, the widows living in quiet houses in forgettable towns, the spinsters dying in dignified silence behind drawn curtains, the last of the old brigade fading into the permanent good-night of the Great War's long shadow.

As the snows of Christmas melted, the Fifth Leicesters were set to work on the new defensive network being built between Béthune and Lens. The coal villages of Beuvry, Cambrin, Annequin, Noyelles and Vermelles were being strengthened with thick belts of wire and machine-gun posts. It was known as the Brown Line. The aim was to contain the German attack inside a battle zone extending to a depth of several miles. Once the German thrust had been blunted inside this zone, it would be driven back. It was an idea already perfected by the Germans. The aim was to out-Hun the Hun. In training, particular stress was laid on platoons and companies working together in the counter-attack. The bayonet came back into favour.

It was like the preparations for the Somme in reverse. Russia's exit from the War had given the Germans enough manpower for a massive attack on the Western Front. The British had been weakened by their losses at Passchendaele and the Prime Minister, David Lloyd George, was deliberately holding reserve divisions in England to prevent Haig undertaking any more costly offensives. The French, whose armies had been racked by mutiny after their own disastrous mistakes in 1917, were considered too fragile to contemplate attacks of their own. Nor could the Allies take too much comfort from the Americans. Millions of them had been promised, but only 175,000 had set foot in France by the beginning of 1918. They were big, strong, well-equipped and useless; they knew nothing about fighting. As a strategist, the American Commander-in-Chief, General John J. Pershing, was a novice. His single big idea was to stay out of combat until a United States Army could take the field as a unified force.

The Allies knew that the German High Command – Hindenburg and Ludendorff – were planning a breakthrough for the spring of 1918, as soon as the ground had dried out, but no one knew where. The French were weaker in morale than the British and therefore the easier target. Yet the French had plenty of room behind them for a fighting withdrawal, and Ludendorff wanted to avoid a protracted engagement. Attrition, at this stage, could only work against him. Germany's Army was supreme in manpower, but its civilian population was on its knees after more than three years of blockade by the Royal Navy. Germany's wretched, starving civilians needed a clinching victory, and quickly. A triumph over the French, however impressive, would not be enough. To win the Great War, Hindenburg and Ludendorff had to deal conclusively with their strongest enemy: England.

At a conference of German warlords on January 21st 1918, Ludendorff announced his grand strategy. His first blow would split the French and British Armies by driving a wedge of infantry at the junction between them. The French would retreat to the south-west in order to protect Paris. The British would retreat to the north-west to protect the Channel ports. Once this rupture had taken place, Ludendorff would feed in his reserves with the immediate aim of encircling the British and pushing them back to the sea. Attacks from the flanks would finish them off. Onward to Victory.

The landscape north and east of Béthune was flat and featureless.

It was ideal cycling country but, unlike the old battlefields of the Somme and the Salient, there were no half-hidden wrinkles suggestive of ancient trench-lines in the fields around Cambrin. My son Gabriel wanted to know what we were doing there, surrounded by turnip tops, shouting '*Bonjour!*' at each passing tractor. According to Hills, the Fifth Leicesters marched into position near Cambrin on March 5th 1918:

> The German offensive was expected to start any day, and the 'wind' was terribly 'up'. This, however, did not prevent the infantry from amusing themselves whenever possible, and though the higher autoritities may have been sleeping in their boots, we managed to get some football.

The Leicesters spent eleven days under intermittent bombard-ment, but there was no all-out infantry attack. There were narrow escapes – one shell crashed through the roof of the HQ dugout and went out of the door without exploding – but no casualties. Many of the German shells were now found to contain gas: green cross for phosgene; blue cross for arsenic; yellow cross for mustard. This latter was the most insidious because it hung around in the cold weather and had no effect until warmed up by the sun, something which might not happen for days. Very little mustard gas was needed to cause blindness, loss of voice and skin blisters. In large doses it was lethal.

On returning to Béthune, the Fifth Leicesters found new battalion badges awaiting them: yellow rings, two inches in diameter, to be sewn on the sleeve at shoulder height. 'They were rather bright at first,' says Hills, 'and earned us the name (among other ruder epithets) of the "Corn-plasters".'

The new fashion in shoulder flashes was yet one more sign of the reorganisation which Haig had ordered in an effort to stretch his forces to meet the German offensive. Starting in January, every infantry brigade had been reduced from four to three battalions. In the 138th (Lincs and Leics) Brigade of the 46th Division, this meant the dissolution of the Fourth Lincolns. The remaining battalions – the Fifth Lincolns, Fourth and Fifth Leicesters – were brought up to strength, and their workload increased accordingly. Another consequence of the Haig reshuffle was a further surplus of Lieutenant-Colonels. Colonel Currin was replaced as C.O. of the Fifth Leicesters by another outsider, Lieutenant-Colonel G.B.G. Wood, D.S.O., of the Lancashire Fusiliers. Major-General Thwaites ordered Wood to have his battalion of yellow arseholes (among other ruder epithets) ready for inspection on the morning of March 22nd. The first blow of Ludendorff's great gamble, *Operation Michael*, was launched against the British on March 21st 1918.

The battle opened at 0440 hours with the biggest artillery bombardment of the War, orchestrated by the supreme German artillerist Georg Bruchmuller, the scourge of Verdun. He had at his disposal over 6,000 guns and 3,000 trench mortars. Instead of a sustained pounding over a wide front, Bruchmuller delivered a series of hammer blows. Five hours after the first guns had fired, mixed cannonades of high explosive and gas merged into a single wall of fire. At 0930 the mortars joined in. Ten minutes later the barrage swept forward, crushing everything in its path.

Ludendorff launched the full weight of *Operation Michael* against that section of the British Line furthest from the coast. Two Armies held this Front: the Third Army, commanded by General Julian Byng; and the Fifth Army, commanded by Sir Hubert Gough. But whereas Byng's Army had to defend a frontage of 28 miles with 14 divisions, Gough had to defend 42 miles with only 15 divisions.

At 0940 hours on Friday, March 21st, 63 German divisions stormed out of the mist into the forward zone of Gough's Fifth Army. With their communications ripped apart by Bruchmuller's bombardment, and with their machine guns blinded by a thick mist, the British stood no chance of co-ordinating an effective resistance. The Germans had been training for months with specially selected groups of storm-troopers. These storm troops – mixed companies of light machine-gunners, bombers and field engineers – advanced at speed to penetrate weaknesses in the British lines, leaving strongpoints to be encircled by the regular infantry following behind.

It was the worst crisis since the retreat from Mons in 1914. By nightfall on March 21st 1918, the British had lost over 38,000 men and nearly 500 guns. Ludendorff boasted that he had inflicted the greatest military defeat in British history. Crown Prince Wilhelm predicted that in 15 days the Germans would be in London. The newspaper *Deutsche Zeitung* gloated over the humiliation of Germany's most hated enemy:

> Away with all petty whining over an agreement and recon-
> ciliation with the fetish of peace. Away with the miserable
> whimpering of those who even now would prevent the
> righteous German hatred of England and sound German
> vengeance.

For Walter and the Fifth Leicesters, stationed just beyond the northernmost point of Ludendorff's battle-front, the first day of *Operation Michael* passed off quietly. The next day, March 22nd, General Thwaites carried out his planned inspection of the Fifth Leicesters as per schedule. Hills said it lasted several hours:

> Our ceremonial was by no means bad. Considering we had

done none for months it was very good. But what most pleased General Thwaites was our organization. In vain he tried to find mistakes. Soldier after soldier was asked 'Who is your Section Commander?' 'Who takes charge if he is killed?' 'When will it be your turn to take charge?' etc, etc. Soldier after soldier answered promptly and correctly. The result was a good word for all of us, and we went back to billets feeling quite elated.

In the space of two weeks, Ludendorff captured more territory than all other commanders on the Western Front in the previous three years. But if he was to land his knock-out punch before Haig could recover, Ludendorff needed to follow the body-blow of *Operation Michael* with a quick left hook. This landed on the eleven miles of British front between La Bassée and Armentières, and once again the Fifth Leicesters found themselves on the edge of the main battle zone, just close enough to feel the shock waves as the blow sent Haig reeling on to the ropes. As Hill's account describes:

On the 8th of April, the enemy's artillery was never silent. Mustard gas was fired into the plain east of Vermelles and Philosophe almost without intermission . . . The following morning in a thick mist the enemy attacked the Portuguese and drove them from their trenches . . . That night we went once more into Brigade support. After relief, Capt. A.G. Moore, M.C., and forty-three other ranks were sent to hospital with gas poisoning . . . For three days we remained in support, and the whole time the plain behind us was full of gas. The artillery suffered most heavily, for they could not always wear their masks, and after the first 24 hours there was a continuous stream of blinded gunners helping each other back . . . On the 12th the battle became quieter, and that night [we were] relieved by the Canadians . . . The Germans had advanced so far that we could see their lights in our left rear. Béthune . . . was in flames.

This German advance north of La Bassée totally changed the shape of the Western Front in Flanders. Previously, the Fifth Leicesters had always faced east; now they faced north, with a huge German army overhanging them like an avalanche poised to fall. The Leicesters' front line, north of the villages of Gorre and Essars, consisted of isolated holes and random slits of trenches. There was no point in developing a system of any permanence. Ludendorff's bid for victory had smashed the old siege lines for good, and there was no telling where he might strike next.

If the Leicesters had been positioned just one mile further north they would have been smashed and scattered as surely as their neighbours. Chance played a part in this deployment, but it was not perhaps the entire explanation. The British Higher Command observed an unofficial order of merit in matching units to particular tasks. At the top of the pecking order were those divisions of the Regular Army which had first crossed to France in 1914. This élite was joined in estimation during 1916 by the Australians and Canadians, whose reputation for hardness and initiative made them the strike-force of choice for most British Army commanders. Next in order of preference came the Kitchener divisions, especially those first-call volunteers who had been blooded during the Somme. Last of all – but still above the Labour Corps and the native troops of the Empire – came the Territorials. On the evidence of their performance at the Hohenzollern Redoubt (complete failure with heavy losses, October 1915) and at Gommecourt (complete failure with heavy losses, July 1916) the Terriers of the 46th Division had been judged to be duffers, fit for quiet sectors like Monchy or diversionary operations like Lens, but last in the queue for any job demanding daring or dash.

Hills and Milne say enough in their respective histories to suggest their bitter frustration at having been weighed in the balance and found wanting. Their failures at the Hohenzollern and Gommecourt had been due to the ineptitude of the Staff rather than any lack of courage in the ranks. As Ludendorff's spring offensives raged nearby, the younger officers of the 46th Division still burned with the desire to prove themselves. In the meantime, while the fate of the Allied cause hung by a thread, the Fifth Leicesters played cricket and practised their breast-stroke in the La Bassée Canal:

> Not only were there constant bathing parties [says Hills], but it was actually possible . . . to hold a swimming gala in the 'Brewery Reach'. There were several well-contested races and diving competitions, uninterrupted by hostile aircraft . . . The chief race was won by Signaller Stanton.

I had expected the La Bassée Canal, a recurring character in many Great War books, to be a placid, rush-fringed backwater brooding over its heroic past. In fact, broad-beamed barges bustled purposefully towards Lille and St Quentin with cargoes of gravel and grain. Hills' photograph – 'The Bathing Pool, Gorre Brewery, 1918' – showed an isolated clump of brick buildings with a high chimney. What remained was a scarred old hulk with most of its windows bricked up. Gorre itself was barely a hamlet at a crossroads. The church on the corner had been rebuilt, and the high wall around the grounds of the old château, but there were no shops, no phone box, not even a bus-stop. There were a few Leicesters in the British cemetery, but none from the Fifth Battalion. I bought Gabriel a cup of hot chocolate in the 'Café Country' and wrote up my epitaphs: 'Gone from our home/But not from our hearts'; 'Until we meet again'; 'Lord, into thy gracious keeping/I leave now/My son is sleeping/Goodnight.'

I peered through the iron gates of the old château, but the driveway led straight into a thick, gloomy wood. Gorre Château and its courtyard full of chestnut trees had gone. I followed the wall to a gate where a hand-written note advertised '*beurre frais et du lait*'. To my left was a range of farm buildings, the château's old stable block. A barking dog alerted the *châtelaine*, who came out wiping her hands on her apron. She brought us into her kitchen, a stone vault full of yellow sunbeams, and gave Gabriel a biscuit.

'*Où est le château?*' I asked.

Madame opened a drawer and brought out a laminated folder of newspaper cuttings and magazine articles. A postcard of the Château de Gorre as it had been during the War showed an unprepossessing two-storey building facing directly on to the road. There was a big gash on the façade and half the roof had been staved-in.

'*Un moment, Madame,*' I said. '*Restez-là!*'

I fumbled in my bag, found Hills' *History Of The Fifth Battalion, The Leicestershire Regiment, T.F.* and quoted aloud:

Both the 4th and 5th Battalions had their Headquarters in the cellar of Gorre Château – cramped and stuffy at any time, and in the hot weather unendurable. Our Headquarters, therefore, cleared out a room on the first floor for a mess. It had a carpet and other luxuries, and its only blemish was a shell-hole in the corner of the window. With great pride we invited Brigadiers and others to our new mess, until on the

17th of May the crash came. The enemy had fired several salvoes towards the Château during the afternoon, and at 8-15 p.m. he started in earnest. The wood, the Château and the corner by the church were shelled unceasingly . . . The mess was knocked in, the wood was filled with gas, the kitchen and signal office both had direct hits . . . General Thwaites was visiting the line at the time and had a narrow escape himself, while his A.D.C. was badly wounded . . .

I tapped Madame's postcard conclusively. That gashed façade and stoved-in roof – we knew how Gorre Château had come by those wounds.

'*Le dix-septième du Mai, Madame. Mon grandpère ici. Beaucoup des obus sur le château. Beaucoup de gaz dans la bois. Très mal.*'

Madame peered over my shoulder as I continued to translate badly from Hills:

We all cleared out and went into the fields, but it was too late . . . Many men's clothes were tainted . . . All the servants and more than half the other Headquarter details were blind . . . The Commanding Officer was unable to speak, the Adjutant half blind and the Padre was doing everybody's job with his wonderful energy . . . It was a very sorrowful Battalion Headquarters that handed over to the Staffordshires and found its way slowly back to Vaudricourt . . .

While Madame made me a little parcel of butter, her son – a medical student on vacation – showed me the yard, pointing out the mossed escutcheons of the Raincheval family and the chiselled keystones which dated the stonework to 1740. After the Great War, he said, the Rainchevals had given up on Gorre. It was too small, too ugly, too badly damaged to be worth repairing;

they'd gone to live in another of their châteaux. I caught a scent of roses and glimpsed the opening scene of some richly textured, Proustian family saga that some other writer would one day try to write about the Great War – and I slammed it shut immediately.

On the morning of June 9th 1918, a patrol of 'D' Company under Second-Lieutenant Maurice 'Bill' Cole went out to investigate the German wire north of Gorre with the aim of snaffling a prisoner. The height of the untended crops in No Man's Land provided cover for what at any other time of the year would have been an exercise in suicidal effrontery. Crawling through the corn, Cole reached a German post established in a deep shell-hole. By a stroke of luck, the sentry was asleep. Cole called up his NCO, Lance-Corporal Thurman, and told him to deal with it:

> The latter [says Hills] hit the sentry on his head with his rifle 'to attract his attention' (so read the patrol report) and leaning over the hole whispered 'Ici yer ——er.' The Boche, however, was too frightened to 'ici' and looked like giving the alarm, so 2nd-Lieut. Cole jumped down and fired his revolver to hurry him along . . . Two German machine-gun posts only a few yards away joined in the fight and for a moment things looked bad for the patrol. The latter, finding they could not get a prisoner, made a note of his regiment, shot him, and made off under heavy fire.

In the entire history of the Fifth Leicesters this is the only record of the direct speech of a private soldier: 'Ici, yer ——er.'

My money's on 'bugger'. Men from Hinckley can barely draw breath without recourse to the B-word. 'Ici, yer bugger,' conveys the exact sardonic tone that Walter would have used as a conversational gambit with a Jerry sentry. But tempting as it was to imagine Walter taking part in the Cole patrol, he probably didn't. The Fifth Leicesters' *War Diary* in the Public Record Office names none of the privates who accompanied Lieutenant Cole. Lance-Corporal Thurman is mentioned in the medical records – on account of the pox he caught in Marseille – but the biggest write-up, naturally, was for the officer. Ten days later Cole was mentioned again after being badly wounded during a sudden German strafe of the trench known as Tuning Fork Switch. He died on June 29th 1918, the day he was awarded the Military Cross for the 'courage, initiative and cunning' he had shown during his Gorre patrol. The only chance Maurice Cole had to wear his medal was on his headstone in Pernes British Cemetery.

Beuvry and Gorre had become the chapter in my Great War book that I wanted to skip. I knew that Walter's War had ended heroically and I was impatient to get there. The Fifth Leicesters had spent seventeen months in the Lens–LaBassée–Béthune sector, during which time they had rarely moved outside an area of seven square miles. I was beginning to feel claustrophobic. I was ardent to tread that battlefield near St Quentin where the 46th Division had amazed the world.

As Ludendorff's juggernaut ran out of steam in Flanders, spring turned into summer and the Allies pulled themselves round for a counter-offensive attack. At Amiens, on August 8th 1918, the tide turned against Germany. For the first time in modern warfare, the British had assembled a force in which all arms – infantry, artillery, armour and aircraft – were co-ordinated to maximum effect. Ludendorff had invented the *blitzkrieg*, but it was the British who perfected it and turned it against him. Two thousand guns opened up at Zero and shepherded the tanks forward behind a creeping barrage. The shock troops following behind – Australians and Canadians – took the German first line within two hours. The artillery then laid down a protective barrage while more tanks were brought up for the next stage. Planes buzzed constantly overhead, spotting targets, relaying information and attacking the Germans whenever opportunity presented. Even the cavalry got their chance, charging over the open fields to harry the German rearguard and seize forward objectives once the German retreat had begun.

As the dust settled, the British could scarcely believe what they had accomplished. Seven hours after Zero, Rawlinson's Fourth Army had gouged a wound in the enemy's flank that was six miles deep and twelve miles wide. Compared with the German attacks of *Operation Michael*, this territorial gain seemed almost modest. But the psychological impact went beyond the numbers of Germans killed, wounded or captured. The ferocity of the British attack, its overwhelming force, the terrifying effect of the massed tanks, all caught the Germans so completely by surprise that many of them fled in panic. Haig wrote to his wife several days afterwards:

> I suppose we have gained the greatest victory which a British Army ever gained . . . But we have not done with the Germans yet . . . the German Army is thoroughly war weary, and our attacks will still go on!

At Gorre and Essars, the 46th Division's plans to withstand another German attack were switched abruptly in the opposite direction. 'Everybody became optimistic,' says Milne. 'The rumour factory went on overtime and the Boches were daily expected to retire, retreat in disorder or lay down their arms.' What Ludendorff actually had in mind was something less dramatic. While some of his divisions had reached breaking point and were fomenting mutiny, the mass of the German army still held together. He ordered a withdrawal to his strongest defensive position – the Hindenburg Line – to allow time for the politicians in Berlin to cobble together some kind of peace settlement.

At this turning point of the War, Major-General Thwaites left the 46th Division to drive a desk in London and was replaced by a much younger man, Major-General G.F. Boyd C.M.G., D.S.O., D.C.M. As usual, it is Milne rather than Hills who captures the spirit of the times:

> Major-General G.F. Boyd had a most attractive personality. He was young. He was handsome. He had gained a commission from the ranks, having won the DCM in the South African War. He had a smile for everyone. He had a brain like lightning and an imagination as vivid . . . When the 46th Division was placed in his hands he seized it as an expert swordsman seizes a priceless blade. This was just the weapon he had been looking for. He would wield it as it had never been wielded before. He would breathe his luck upon it; with it he would leap to victory.

And, astoundingly, that is how it turned out. The lumpen Terriers of the 46th Division were about to achieve one of the most astonishing feats of arms accomplished by the British during the Great War. At midnight on September 11th 1918, the Fifth Leicesters formed up on the parade ground of the barracks in Béthune – now a sad ruin of a town – and marched to the railway station, bound for glory.

Before leaving, I wanted to pay my respects to Lieutenant Cole. The little market town where he'd died, Pernes, was 13 winding

miles from the trenches where he'd been wounded. I found him
in a shallow valley on the outskirts of town where the British had
pitched their tented hospital. The War Cemetery was a Lutyens
design, made interesting by an oblique approach through a fragrant
mass of white roses. My wife found a green nook to rest in while
the children and I fanned out through the dazzling ranks of white
headstones. We could have gone straight to the cemetery register,
but I always felt it more satisfying to find Leicesters by instinct.
Lieutenant Cole was second from the end of a row near the top
of the field.

'Who was he?' asked Phoebe.

'He was one of my grandad's officers. Perhaps.'

I told Phoebe the story of how Cole and his men had sneaked
out through the corn to snare them a German prisoner.

'And they killed him?'

'They had to.'

I took out my notebook and began to copy the inscription
that Cole's parents had chosen for him.

'But you said the German was asleep.'

Second Lieutenant Wm. Maurice Cole, MC.

'He woke up,' I said, 'and shouted to his friends.'

29th June 1918.

'So they killed him?'

'They had to. The Germans had machine guns.'

His love for his family.

'Where's the German buried?'

His life for his country.

'We never go to German cemeteries,' insisted Phoebe.

His soul for God.

'Look,' I said, 'the Germans killed him—'

I steered Phoebe's attention not to Maurice Cole's headstone
but to the one next to it, marking the grave of Private John

Frederick Power of the Suffolk Regiment. The inscription had been partly obscured by dust, so I helped my daughter to trace the letters with her finger-tip.

'*In loving memory of my brave daddy.*'

10

PONTRUET

> . . . *I'm blind with tears,*
> *Staring into the dark. Cheerho!*
> *I wish they'd killed you in a decent show.*
> Siegfried Sassoon, 'To any Dead Officer'

A fter the Amiens victory of August 8th, the imperative for the Allies was to keep up the pressure. The Allied *generalissimo*, Ferdinand Foch, proposed hitting the Germans on so many fronts that they would never be able to recover. There would be four consecutive offensives at the end of September. The first would involve the French and the Americans in the south; they would push the Germans back in the Argonne. The second attack would bring in the British First and Third Armies; they would attack towards Cambrai. The third attack would combine the British and Belgian forces in Flanders; they would keep the Germans off balance on the flank. The fourth attack would be the knock-out, smashing straight through the centre of the Germans' most formidable position, the Hindenburg Line. It was envisaged that this attack, spearheaded by the British Fourth Army with support from the Americans, would be followed by a general collapse of German resistance.

By the time these plans were ready, the Germans had pulled back on a broad front and were manning the Hindenburg Line in strength. First used in the German withdrawal of March 1917, the Hindenburg Line was the longest and strongest defensive feature of the whole Western Front. It stretched from Arras in the north to Soissons in the south, a distance of some 60 miles. Its forward zone consisted of sentry posts and concrete dugouts. Companies of men were meant to shelter in these dugouts during the preliminary bombardment and then come out to attack advancing Allied infantry in the rear. Behind this forward area came the main battle zone, more than a mile deep, where the trench systems were reinforced with concrete blockhouses sited for mutual cover by machine guns. Behind this battle zone came the support lines where reserves were held ready for immediate counter-attack. Throughout the system, thick belts of barbed wire had been so placed as to shepherd attackers into killing zones covered by machine guns and artillery. The Hindenburg Line was considered by the Germans to be impregnable. To reach it, the British had to haul themselves across country ravaged by four years of warfare. It cost them another 180,000 casualties and immense expenditure of effort, but they fought doggedly forward until they were within striking distance.

Sir Douglas Haig, who up until this point had spent most of his War at Montreuil (closer to Dover than the nearest trenches) now shifted his headquarters to a train so that he could follow preparations in detail. He is credited with sensing the possibility of victory at an earlier stage than most Allied commanders, probably because he had a keener perception of the true balance of forces. If the Germans were to be beaten in 1918 it was the British who would have to do it. The Americans had the numbers, but not the experience; the French had the experience, but not the energy. As Ludendorff had perceived, and as Haig had argued all along, the Great War resolved itself in the end into a straightforward fight between Britain and Germany on the Western Front.

By the last week in September, the British had pushed forward until they were well within range of Cambrai. To the south, where the main attack was scheduled for September 29th, the most difficult stretch of the Hindenburg Line remained intact. Here, the Germans had incorporated the St Quentin Canal into the very heart of their defences. And what made this section even more formidable was a three-mile-long tunnel between the villages of Bellenglise and Vendhuille. This tunnel was safe from all artillery and served the Germans as a subterranean fortress connected to forward and support trenches by bomb-proof passages. Thousands of men based in the tunnel could be moved quickly to any part of the line under attack. Villages in the area had been further strengthened to command the best fields of fire. It was here, between the tunnel and the village of Bellenglise, that the canal cutting was deepest and the British would face the fiercest resistance.

The commander of the Fourth Army, Sir Henry Rawlinson, had assigned the most difficult part of the attack – crossing the canal – to the British IX Corps commanded by Lieutenant-General Braithwaite. General Braithwaite delegated the task to the 46th Division, led by that dashing newcomer Major-General Boyd. If Boyd succeeded, Braithwaite would be lauded as a shrewd judge of character. If Boyd failed, it wouldn't matter much because nobody was expecting a victory from the Terriers. The worst that could happen was that they would botch the job with heavy casualties, as usual. Even that would serve to soften up the Germans for a more considered effort by the élite troops of the 1st or 6th Divisions.

The Fifth Leicesters went into trenches opposite the St Quentin Canal on September 21st 1918. They had Americans and Australians on their left and the British 1st Division on their right. The Americans had done well to establish themselves in the outlying trenches of the Hindenburg Line, but in their inexperience they'd pushed too far ahead. They occupied high ground overlooking the St Quentin Canal, and they could see the main Hindenburg strongholds on the other side. Their right flank, however, was up in the air and exposed to enfilade fire from a village called Pontruet, which was still in German hands. General Boyd's first task was to nip out Pontruet and straighten his line so that his stab across the canal could go in clean and true. General Boyd gave the job to Brigadier Rowley of the 138th (Lincs and Leics) Brigade, who assigned it to the Fifth Leicesters. It was the moment Hills had been waiting for since the beginning of the War: a straight fight for a clear-cut objective, with the whole British Army watching.

Frontal attacks on Pontruet had already been shown to be unworkable in battalion strength, so the plan was for the Fifth Leicesters to attack from the flank and storm the Germans from behind. They would advance downhill from the American-held ridge behind a creeping barrage. The line of this advance lay parallel to a strong German trench, identified on British maps as Forgan's Trench. When they reached Pontruet, 'A' and 'B' Companies would wheel right and enter the village while 'D' Company would wheel left and deal with Forgan's Trench. 'C' company would go wherever they seemed to be needed most. Once Pontruet had been entered, platoons would split up into sections to winkle out resistance with the bomb and the bayonet. Headquarters would stay on the high ground in the hope of maintaining signal contact. Zero was set for 0500 hours, September 24th.

It took the Fifth Leicesters six days to get from Béthune to Pontruet, travelling by troop-train and open lorry. It was a miserable journey. The retreating Germans had left nothing behind. Farmhouses had been blown up, barns torched and wells poisoned with ordure and corpses. The most fertile landscape in France had been turned into a black wilderness.

We covered the same distance in under an hour, the woods and villages of the Santerre unfolding like a quilt of prosperity. The municipal camp-site at St Quentin was positively luxurious, with hot running water at no extra charge. While my wife went to forage, I cycled to the ridge where the Fifth Leicesters had assembled for their assault on Pontruet. Hills' sketch map of the battle showed the exact dispositions of the four companies of the Fifth Leicesters on Tuesday, September 24th 1918.

The Fifth Leicesters paraded for battle at midnight after dumping their greatcoats and swigging down an issue of hot tea and rum. When they arrived at their jumping-off line on top of the ridge, they found that some Germans were indeed still occupying the trench – Forgan's Trench – which the Americans on the left had occupied as their outpost line. This German presence meant that 'D' Company, which had been assigned to the left flank of the attack, was not able to assemble in the open with the other three companies but was inside that unoccupied section of Forgan's Trench between the Germans and the Americans. Hills says that, apart from some scattered shelling in the early hours, all was quiet:

In absolute silence we lay in shell holes waiting for Zero. A

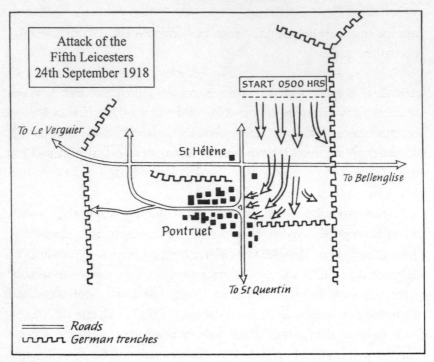

Attack of the
Fifth Leicesters
24th September 1918

START 0500 HRS

To Le Verguier

St Hélène

To Bellenglise

Pontruet

To St Quentin

===== Roads
ᴜᴜᴜᴜ German trenches

mist had started to blow up from the valley, and the Battalion
was almost invisible. Here and there a few heads, the muzzle
of a Lewis gun, the end of a stretcher, might be seen just
above ground, and occasionally one could see the tall figure
of Captain Tomson, imperturbable as ever, walking quietly
round his Company [B] with a word of encouragement for all.
As the time went on, the mist became thicker and thicker. By
4-50 a.m. platoons and Companies were unable to see each
other . . . it was very quiet.

At 0500 hours, the British barrage opened with a crash and the Fifth
Leicesters jumped from cover. Following close behind the curtain
of bursting shells they marched downhill until, at the bottom of the
slope, they came to the straight road leading to the canal crossing
at Bellenglise about half a mile to their left. In front of them,

196

some 250 yards across this road and still hidden in the mist, was Pontruet.

By 0514 hours, most of the Fifth Leicesters had crossed the road and were ready for their next move. It was still half-dark and visibility was further hindered by a smoke barrage laid down by the artillery in spite of a specific request to the contrary. 'A' Company wheeled right in parade-ground style and plunged into the gloom:

> Odd lengths of trenches and cellars in every direction were filled with [German] bombers and machine-gun teams . . . Led by Lieut Brodribb and their platoon commanders, A Company dashed in with the bayonet. Here and there a bomb was thrown down a cellar, or a Lewis gun turned against some party which resisted, but for the most part the bayonet was the weapon of the day. The enemy were scattered, a few tried to fight, but large numbers were killed trying to escape, while 120 were captured, and 50 more were driven into the Sherwood Foresters' lines . . . The Company's heaviest losses were in the southern side of the village [where] the Germans had two lengths of well-defended trench, supported by a blockhouse. Against these 2nd-Lieuts. Aster and Quint and Corporal Tyers led their men. The two officers were killed almost together at the second trench, but the Corporal broke clean through, only to be shot through the head when almost outside the village. Seven others of this same gallant party were killed at this corner . . .

The problem was the fog, compounded by the smoke barrage. The platoons of 'B' Company in the centre of the attack lost touch with each other. One platoon stumbled after 'A' Company and was cut up by the German machine guns in the blockhouse.

Another platoon came adrift because its subaltern, Cosgrove, could see so little that he had to stop every few yards to take compass bearings. Meanwhile, the Germans in Forgan's Trench had been wreaking destruction. Instead of being held by a few isolated posts, as expected, Forgan's was held in strength: 'It was wired in front and lateral belts had been placed at frequent intervals across it. It would have been a stiff task for a Company to take it with a frontal assault; to "work up" it was impossible. None the less D Company did their utmost.'

It was a futile utmost. The Germans had a nest of three machine guns where Forgan's Trench intersected with the Bellenglise road. As 'D' Company, with Walter in it, came down the hill these three machine guns opened up with 'a perfect hurricane of bullets'. Captain Brooke tried to rush the position but was hit three times and had to be carried away. The rear platoons of 'D' Company dropped down into the trench to take cover. Lieutenant Corah came up to take command but too late, for the men had lost momentum and had gone to ground. 'D' Company was so effectively pinned down that it was out of the fight for the rest of the day.

'C' Company did manage to cross the road and reach the village where, despite 'A' Company having passed through, there were still Germans firing from positions along the eastern boundary. Lieutenant Hawley attacked them, turned them out and occupied a trench facing east towards Forgan's. A separate party, led by Lieutenant Barrett, stumbled straight ahead instead of turning right and ended up in a German trench that hadn't been marked on any of the British maps:

This puzzled him [says Hills]. The trench had been newly dug during the night but as it was full of Germans, he rushed it, got inside, and turned towards Forgan's. He was hit doing so. Reaching Forgan's, this party, in which Sergeant Spencer was conspicuous, quickly disposed of three German machine-gun posts and their teams, but were then themselves fired at and bombed from several directions. Undeterred, Lieut. Barrett, though again wounded, drew his revolver and held up one bombing party while Sergeant Spencer dealt with another. A bomb burst close to Lieut. Barrett's pistol arm and put it out of action. By this time he was becoming exhausted. Calling his NCOs together, he explained what had happened and gave them careful directions as to how to get out, himself quite calm the whole time. Acting on his instructions, those of the party who were left cut their way out. Lieut. Barrett, refusing help, started to crawl through the wire and was again wounded. He eventually reached the Regimental Aid Post literally covered with wounds.

While this was going on, Captain Tomson of 'B' Company was groping around in the fog trying to find his men. All he had with him were his runners, his company signallers and a few batmen. In desperation he rounded them up and decided to attack the nearest German position, which happened to be a machine-gun post in Forgan's:

His little party forced their way through some wire and found themselves opposed by three guns. With a shout of 'Come along Tigers, show them what you can do,' Captain Tomson led them straight at the enemy. Two of the gun teams were overcome, but the third could not be reached and fired at them point blank. Lance Corporal Signaller J. Smith was wounded and fell, Captain Tomson, bending down to tie him up was shot through the head. Only two men got away, leaving their leader, now dead, in a small shelter outside the trench. Smith, mortally wounded, refused to be taken away, saying, 'Leave me with Captain Tomson, I shall be all right' – and there he died.

By 0630 hours it was full daylight, but Hills and the rest of Battalion HQ on top of the ridge could see nothing because of the fog and smoke. It was not until 0745 hours that a wind blew up and revealed the progress of the battle. The village of Pontruet, with the exception of the blockhouse at the south-west corner, appeared to have been taken. Parties of 'C' Company were assumed to be holding the eastern edge; 'A' and 'B' had dug in on the north-west corner; another party had dug in at the cemetery. The road leading west from the village was 'thronged with prisoners and stretcher bearers making their way towards the large crater on the main road, used as a Company Headquarters by the Sherwood Foresters'.

In Forgan's Trench, however, there was deadlock. With the Germans holding the trench in force beyond the Bellenglise road, 'D' Company remained pinned down within a couple of hundred yards of where they'd started. Now that the smoke had dissipated, any movement from them brought down instant machine-gun fire. It was here, in Forgan's Trench, that I had hoped to find Walter.

I went downhill, following the exact line of the Leicesters' attack. When I got to the Bellenglise road I stopped and walked west until I reached a junction marked on Hills' sketch map as Ste Hélène crossroads. This was my fixed point. I turned east, squared my shoulders and began pacing along the road towards Bellenglise, counting my steps as I went. According to Hills' map, the line of Forgan's Trench ran some 550 yards to the east.

I knew what I was going to find, but I counted the distance

anyway. After 547 paces I found myself in a concrete underpass. Above me was the south-bound carriageway of the A26–E17 autoroute, the same road which had obliterated Walter's trench at Vimy Ridge. I pressed my palm to the wall of the underpass and absorbed the vibrations of the traffic rumbling overhead. Some surveyor had painted the figure '558' on the wall, presumably the precise number of metres to the Ste Hélène crossroads.

I felt stupid, like a man who had walked into the same joke twice on the same day. Somewhere under the tonnes of concrete and asphalt around me lay the remains of the trench where I had hoped to find Walter. The same new motorway which had thwarted me at Vimy Ridge had done it again. How many motorways did Europe need? Once again I felt an awareness of how small I was, an English speck upon the sprawling geography of Europe. And there it was again, that nagging ambivalence about Germany – how close it was, how strong, how inescapable.

I headed for the village of Pontruet, kicking through the tangled vines and dusty stalks of a pea field that had been recently harvested. The spilled peas which had dried in the sun were the size and colour of shrapnel rounds. I kicked up a rusty shell splinter, looked for more and found them, confirming that I was close to Walter and the Fifth Leicesters. Certainty may have eluded me at Forgan's Trench, but the battle wasn't over yet.

The stalemate in Forgan's Trench was not the main obstacle to the Leicesters' attack; the real problem was the German blockhouse in the south-west corner of the village. A tank from the 1st Division tried to deal with it, but broke down before it could get within range and was soon put out of action by German artillery. Brigadier Rowley began to fret. He wanted Pontruet in the bag by nightfall. A new artillery barrage was out of the question since nobody knew exactly where the Leicesters already in Pontruet were sheltering. But another infantry attack was feasible, and the Brigadier ordered the Sherwood Foresters to lend the Leicesters enough men to carry it out.

At 1930 hours, as darkness closed in, the second assault began. The first attack had been conceived as a sweep through the village from east to west; the second was a sweep from north to south. Once again the attackers had trouble trying to keep in touch, this time because of the darkness and the wreckage caused by the earlier battle:

> A Company's left kept close to the Sherwood Foresters, but the outer flanks of both were 'in the air', for C Company could not be found. It was dark when the south side of the village was reached . . . A Lewis Gun Section, under C.S.M. Wardle disposed of the only party of enemy who were encountered, but the post near the blockhouse could not be found . . . We had accomplished nothing.

To add to the ignominy, the battalion due to relieve the Leicesters – Sherwood Foresters, presumably, although Hills diplomatically omits to specify – refused to take over because the position around Pontruet was in such a mess. Having fought all day, the men of 'A' and 'B' Companies were too tired to make another attempt at forming a line around the village. 'C' Company, when it was finally located, was too far away to link up with the others. 'D' Company was still in Forgan's Trench.

At 0200 hours on September 25th, the Fifth Leicesters were ordered to evacuate:

> What was left of the Battalion then marched back to where we had left our greatcoats, while the Sherwood Foresters took

over the line north and west of Pontruet. The Adjutant saw
the last parties out of the village, and the Colonel, though
tired out, insisted on going round the lines and visiting each
platoon as it came in.

The cost in Fifth Leicesters' officers of not securing Pontruet was
three killed and seven wounded. The cost in other ranks was 30
killed, 100 wounded and eight missing.

Major-General Boyd sent a message to Brigadier Rowley the
next day, asking him to congratulate the Leicesters on the 'good
fight' they had put up:

> Owing to unexpected reinforcements, they attacked an
> enemy twice as strong as themselves, and moreover in a
> strong position. Although we did not reach our objective,
> the enemy was prevented from reinforcing the troops opposed
> to the Division on our right.

Hills' verdict, in trying too hard to sound positive, merely empha-
sises the sad extent of the failure:

> We had proved that five platoons could clear a village held
> by three Battalions (so said one of the prisoners) . . . We had
> shown that when NCO's became casualties, private soldiers
> were ready to assume command and become leaders . . . Most
> important of all, the battle had proved to each individual
> soldier that if he went with his bayonet he was irresistible.

It was a pretty bleak achievement, though there was one consolation. Lieutenant Barrett was awarded the Victoria Cross and
eventually made a complete recovery.

★   ★   ★

There is a photograph of Pontruet in Hills' book, showing a tall crucifix among the weed-infested wreckage of the village cemetery. I went to the place marked on Hills' map, but discovered that the graves had all been relocated to a more spacious site beyond the village. The base of the crucifix remained, however, and was the main feature of a little square of gravel marked out for boules and named after René Boitelle (1921–1986). I hunkered down for my traditional few moments of introspection close to the earth. On September 24th 1918, Corporal Barber had been here with a few men of 'A' Company. Had anyone from Leicester been here since? Was I the first, or the three-hundred-and-first? My feelings were strong, but the meaning of the battle for Pontruet remained out of reach. Some words had survived on the base of the crucifix: '*Je suis la résurrection et la vie.*'

The lane by which we left Pontruet was splashed with clods of manure and squashed potatoes. We stopped at the Mairie-Ecole. The bus-stop and graffiti-scarred telephone kiosk outside confirmed that, in so far as there was communal life, this was its epicentre. Most of the documents on the notice-board were applications for building permits, stamped with flamboyantly signatured endorsements. Citizens were reminded of their obligations relating to communal sewerage and the need for prompt registration of guns held for '*La Chasse*'. The Fifth Leicesters had fought for Pontruet so that its inhabitants might observe due legal process in seeking to extend their outhouses.

As we headed for the canal crossing at Bellenglise, whooshing under the motorway that had obliterated Forgan's Trench, I said over my shoulder, 'Grandad was here, Phoebe, a long time ago.'

'Where?'

She was bored with Walter's War. She liked picnics and speaking little bits of French in *boulangeries*. She liked climbing trees at the camp-site. She thought my interest in monuments and cemeteries was silly.

'He spent all day in a trench under this road,' I said.

'Under it?'

We had left the motorway behind already.

'Grandad and his friends were at one end of the trench, the Germans were at the other.'

'Under the motorway?'

'Before it was built,' I said. 'During the War.'

I could see that, from a certain point of view, it didn't make a great deal of sense.

11

VICTORY

You whom the kings saluted; who refused not
The one great gesture of ignoble days,
Fame without name and glory without gossip . . .
    G.K. Chesterton, 'To the Unknown Soldier'

In spite of his polite message to the Fifth Leicesters, their rebuff at Pontruet had given General Boyd a real problem. The point he'd selected for his attack on the Hindenburg Line was the mile of the St Quentin Canal between Bellenglise and the Riqueval Bridge, the only bridge across the canal capable of carrying wheeled traffic. At Bellenglise the canal was described as 'dry' – that is, most of the water had drained away leaving the canal bed full of sticky ooze. At Riqueval, however, where artillery fire had done less damage, the water was still six feet deep. Getting the 46th Division across this vexing obstacle was Boyd's primary concern. The canal lay at the bottom of a deep embankment between sheer sides. Crossing it, however that was to be done, would have to be accomplished in the face of point-blank fire from massed machine guns. Only when the 46th Division had reached the eastern bank of the St Quentin Canal would they be able to attack the Hindenburg Line proper. The failure at Pontruet meant that Boyd had to find another way to widen his jumping-off zone on the canal's west bank. At 1600 hours on Friday, September 27th, the Fourth Leicesters were delegated to carry out this operation. Their first inkling of it was when the Colonel arrived at 'A' Company HQ waving a large map. His orders were to attack Peg Copse and Pike Wood behind a creeping barrage in three hours' time.

At 1900 hours, the barrage opened and the four companies of the Fourth Leicesters began their advance. According to Milne, the Germans were taken completely by surprise:

> Numbers 1, 2, and 3 platoons of A Company reached their objective without a shot being fired . . . The barrage had kept the Germans in their deep dugouts . . . They surrendered freely without putting up much fight . . . Number 4 platoon met with some resistance, and they killed quite a number of the enemy in hand to hand fighting, but Lieut. Partridge and Sergeant Hemmings soon cleared the trench, and one German was so anxious to surrender that he flung his arms around Partridge's neck begging for mercy. Captain Pick, who happened to come down the trench at this embarrassing moment, curtly asked his subaltern what he was 'playing at'.

With 'A' Company in Peg Copse and 'B' Company in Pike Wood, the evening's work should have been over. The two support companies rapidly established communications along the length of the new line, and by 1945 hours two German officers and 150 men had been sent back as prisoners. All that remained was for the Fourth Leicesters to hand over to the Staffords as planned. Unfortunately, the Staffords of 137th Brigade could not be found. Milne describes how the Fourth Leicesters' successful little attack soon degenerated into a desperate holding operation as the Germans tried to fight their way back:

> The enemy had now recovered from his surprise and was pushing up strong parties along trenches leading from the canal. All night long they tried to bomb their way back into their old position but without success ... If it had not been for the extraordinary good show put up by the Battalion the position would have been lost, and this might have seriously hindered subsequent operations. At last, when dawn was breaking, the Fifth and Sixth North Staffords arrived (carrying ladders and wearing lifebelts) and relieved the weary companies ... The Battalion had advanced 700 yards on a 500-yard front, taken 150 prisoners, and with both flanks in the air had held the position until relieved. It was a bloody little fight of which any regiment might well be proud.

The Staffords arrived late carrying ladders and wearing life-belts because they had been taken 12 miles back to Brie, on the River Somme, for a canal-crossing rehearsal. They had also been given bulky coir mats to smooth their passage across the muddy stretches of the canal, and collapsible boats for the watery bits. Even as the Staffords assembled, guns of all calibres were still being hauled into position behind them. Every spinney, hedge or ruin that could be screened from the enemy was being turned into a gun-pit or supply dump.

The full details of General Boyd's plan were spelled out to the Leicesters at Brigade HQ on the morning of Saturday,

September 28th 1918. The attack against the Hindenburg Line would open at dawn the next day with a hurricane bombardment across the whole front. The heaviest calibres would pound the main positions to keep the Germans deep in their underground bunkers. Simultaneously, a creeping barrage would register just ahead of the British front line. As soon as this barrage moved off, the Staffords would advance behind it to the St Quentin Canal. Once they'd slithered down the west bank of the cutting, crossed the canal and clambered up the east bank, they would regroup in the shelter of the barrage and follow it once more – right into the main trench of the Hindenburg Line. Once they had seized this trench, some 1,000 yards east of the canal, the Staffords would consolidate while the barrage marked time in order for tanks to be brought up. This was the cue for the Leicesters to enter the scene. Once the tanks were ready, the Leicesters would cross the canal by whatever means were available, form up behind the barrage and 'pass through' the Staffords, aiming for the high ground around the fortified village of Magny la Fosse. This line, marked on the maps in green ink, was the Fifth Leicesters' final objective. If they reached it, they would have broken through. Staffords + Leicesters = Breakthrough. Onward to Victory.

The Fifth Leicesters spent Saturday preparing in detail. Their advance would consist of 'A' Company on the right, 'C' Company in the centre and 'D' Company on the left. The commanders of these companies held a conference with the crews of the tanks which had been assigned to their line of advance. Once they'd agreed times and map references, they went back to brief their men. It was imperative for infantry and armour to stick precisely to the artillery timetable; each 'lift' in the barrage had been worked out to the minute. If the infantry came adrift from the protective screen of shellfire, the attack would be lost.

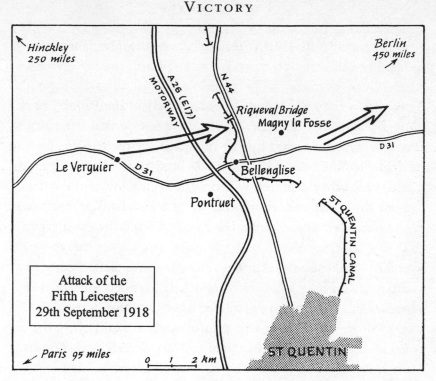

Attack of the
Fifth Leicesters
29th September 1918

Towards evening the rain which had fallen intermittently all day eased off, giving the prospect of fine weather. Bombs and flares were issued. Each man was given two water bottles, plus an extra day's ration in addition to his iron ration. Then he tried to sleep. Hills says it was a quiet night. Milne says the darkness throbbed with the continual sound of guns, tanks, pontoons and supply parties moving into position.

At 0550 hours on Sunday, September 29th, the battle began. Milne writes:

Every Allied gun within miles belched. Dante's Inferno was a mere twitter to this. This was the real thing; there were no two ways about it, this was quite definitely fiery bloody Hell. Hell let loose on earth. Hell with a capital H. Hell

211

with the lid off. Heart-breaking, body-rending, shrieking, blasting HELL.

There was a thick mist, but this time it helped the British. As the barrage from Hell began to move towards the Germans, the British first waves, encumbered by life-belts and life-jackets, formed up in lines:

Following close on the barrage the Staffords captured the trenches west of the canal. Here [says Milne] the enemy put up a stout resistance, but the fog was thick, the barrage was sudden and the Staffords were not stopping for anything or anyone. On they went with reddened bayonets, leaving any remaining Germans to the tender mercies of the moppers-up. Down the canal bank they poured and crossed as best they could. In some places the canal was dry and the passage was easy; in others there was several feet of water, and life-belts, life-lines, and rafts were used. Some crossed by a concrete dam, some by Ricqueval [sic] Bridge which was captured in the nick of time as the enemy was about to blow it sky high. The fog still held, thickened by the smoke of the barrage. The machine-gun posts on the east of the canal were rushed and the teams bayoneted. The trenches near the canal bank were captured, and the enemy infantry, bewildered by the suddenness of the barrage and the fury of the attack, surrendered in hundreds; they put up but a poor fight. After checking to re-organise their men the Staffords swept on to their final objective 1,000 yards east of the canal which had been designated the Brown Line. Here they halted and consolidated the position. They were well up to time and had captured their objective in two hours and thirty minutes. The fog had been a godsend but it had made keeping position difficult. They were superbly led. The gunners' shooting had been excellent. The Staffords had taken over two thousand prisoners. Their own losses were twenty-five officers and five hundred men. The Staffordshire Terrier is a fine fighting breed.

In actual fact Milne could have seen none of it. The two Leicester battalions were at least a mile away when the Staffords went into action. According to Hills:

There was the usual thick morning mist, and even at 7-0 a.m. we were unable to see more than a few yards in any direction. Even gun flashes could not be seen, and the only intimation we had of the progress of the fight, was the continuous 'chug-chug-chug' of the tanks, moving along the valley north of us completely out of sight. As we were not due to move until 9-0 a.m. we spent the time having breakfasts.

Seeing that the mist wasn't dissipating, Brigade HQ ordered an advance. At 0830 hours the Fifth Leicesters lined up beside the old quarry that had been their headquarters:

The mist was so thick one could not see from one end of a Company to the other and it was nearly nine o'clock before [the Medical Officer] Captain Jack and his orderlies with their medical box appeared in the field . . .

Soon after setting off in single file, with the Colonel at the head of 'A' Company, an artillery column moving back to re-supply cut the Fifth Leicesters in half. What happened next was a classic illustration of how easily things could go amiss in the fog of war:

Alongside us, moving on the same track, were the Fifth

Sherwood Foresters, also bound for the Green Line; their
'all up' was passed to the head of our column, and the
Colonel, thinking we were intact, moved on . . . Eventually,
after crossing the old front line and going half way down the
next slope, the Colonel halted, and allowing the Companies
to form up by platoons, waited until it was time to go on.
He judged that he should be somewhere near the starting
line of the Staffordshires. C and D Companies came up but
there was no Battalion Headquarters and no B Company
. . . Fortunately, at 10-45 the mist blew right away, and
the sudden daylight which followed showed him where the
Battalion lay; it also showed the Staffordshires' starting tape
only 60 yards from where the Colonel had halted.

Shortly before 1200 hours the artillery barrage for the advance of
the 138th Brigade began. The Fourth Leicesters were in front,
followed by the Fifth Lincolns, followed by the Fifth Leicesters:

On reaching the canal [says Hills], the two right Companies
[A and C] crossed by the remains of an old dam, the left [D]
by Riquerval [sic] Bridge . . . all formed up in the remains
of the famous Hindenburg Line on the far side. It had been
terribly battered, and here and there the remains of its occupants
showed how deadly our barrage, and how fierce the assault of
the Staffordshires had been. As we reached the canal a single
tank was seen coming down from the north, another followed
and then others. Our Battalion [of tanks] had crossed successfully
at Bellicourt, so the battle must be going well.

Having linked up with their tanks as per schedule, the Fifth
Leicesters headed for the Green Line, with the village of Magny

la Fosse at its centre. Hills says the advance was accomplished in textbook style. The Colonel led the way with his eye firmly fixed on Magny village:

> Behind him, the three Companies deployed [with] their 'distance' and 'interval' perfect . . . if one was checked for a time, the others saw it at once and conformed . . . Swarms of prisoners, waving their arms, were seen coming from various trenches . . . no-one was looking after them, we were all much too keen on getting forward. Here and there, when a few Boches showed signs of getting into a trench instead of keeping to the open, some soldier would administer a friendly jab with the bayonet to show what was expected of them.

The Fifth Leicesters pushed through Magny la Fosse and by 1340 hours were only 600 yards from their final objective, Fosse Wood. The British artillery was firing at almost the limit of its range by this stage, and some guns were shooting short. 'A' Company reached its objective first and made its headquarters in a sunken road. 'C' Company advanced next, reached a ruined mill and linked up with 'A' Company's outposts. Walter and 'D' Company on the left reached Fosse Wood in time to capture a German artillery officer and 50 men before they could escape with their battery of field guns. Nearby, they surprised another bunch of Germans trying to blow up a howitzer. Altogether, 'D' Company captured eight guns. They chalked their names on their trophies, sent back their prisoners and dug in.

Whoever held the Riqueval Bridge held the Hindenburg Line. Whoever held the Hindenburg Line, held the Western Front. By taking the bridge and breaking the Line, the 46th Division won the Great War. Or at least, that's one way of looking at it.

It was the capture of the Riqueval Bridge by a company of the Sixth North Staffords that unlocked the battle. They were led by Captain A.H. Charlton, who like many commanders that day had led his men through the fog by compass. As they slid down the bank on the western side of the bridge they were spotted and fired at. Captain Charlton charged. The bridge's German demolition squad leapt from their hiding-place but were killed before they could detonate their hidden explosives. The Staffords stormed across the bridge and cleared the enemy from the trenches and blockhouses on the eastern side. I walked in the opposite direction, past the concrete stump of the blockhouse remaining, and stood at the place on the bridge from which Brigadier J.V. Campbell V.C. had addressed his Staffords after the battle. The photograph of him leaning against a wobbly bit of the parapet remains the greatest image of victory in the whole of the Great War: Campbell half turns towards the photographer with the suggestion of a satisfied expression on his handsome old face; behind him, completely covering the impossibly steep incline, swarm hundreds of Staffords cheering for posterity, some of them still wearing the life-vests in which they first crossed the canal.

On Sunday, September 29th 1918, between 11.30 a.m. and 12.30 p.m., Private Walter Butterworth of 'D' Company, Fifth Battalion, the Leicestershire Regiment, slid down a slight incline from a beet field, leapt over a captured German trench and crossed the Riqueval Bridge from west to east.

The bridge was the specific point of the Western Front – date, time and grid reference – that I had set out to find. I felt satisfaction rather than triumph. Canals are mysterious, they move but they don't flow. Whatever falls into a canal stays there. This canal was green and gloomy and eerily quiet. No barges had reason to come this way, no dog-owners whistled in the undergrowth. There was nothing to disturb my thoughts of Walter and how, once upon a time, his shadow had fallen, exactly like mine, from the Riqueval Bridge into the St Quentin Canal.

I looked though my camera and took the photograph so obligingly provided by natural symmetry. The surface of the canal reflected a rectangle of blue sky bisected by the pretty white arch I was standing on. Underneath, hidden for ever beneath the ooze, lay bones and battle debris. I tried to imagine the scene as it would have looked when Walter and 'D' Company passed over into the reeking remains of the Hindenburg Line. This was the place I had been looking for all right. I had found Walter, but this was not the place to say goodbye. I got on my bike and headed for the Green Line.

The hamlet of Magny la Fosse consisted of three farms and a signpost to the next village, Le Haucourt. Magny's entire population during the Great War could not have exceeded half-a-dozen families, yet the War Memorial at the cross-roads (*'Aux enfants de Magny la Fosse morts pour la France*, 1914–1918') bore eight names. At the topmost farm I explained that I was a student of the Great War looking for clues. A tractor driver took me to a corner of the yard where some monstrous old shells lay in a rusty heap, like dinosaur eggs. I left my bike and went forward on foot.

My destination was Fosse Wood, where Walter and 'D' Company had found the Germans trying to blow up their howitzer. I plunged into the wood and stopped in my tracks. In a mossed declivity in the centre of the copse, dappled by sunlight and bound tight with ivy, lay several amputated torsos – chunks of concrete from some wrecked blockhouse or gun-pit. They sprawled like untended corpses – stiff, abandoned, somehow imploring. Something evil had happened in Fosse Wood, and this was the testimony.

Hills says that when 'D' Company under Lieutenant Corah reached Fosse Wood and found twenty Germans trying to blow up their howitzer, 'they demonstrated that this could not be allowed and took them all prisoner.' Of what force and violence was that demonstration? With nothing more to support me than a spooky feeling on the back of my neck, I was willing to believe that 'D' Company had dispensed summary justice to their German saboteurs. 'Without further opposition,' says Hills, '[D Company] dug in round the east side of the wood and continued the line northwards to the Divisional boundary.'

I hunkered down for communion with the earth. For a brief moment in this place, Walter and his comrades had comprised the bayonet-tip of the British Army on the offensive. For an hour or two on the evening of September 29th 1918, in the copse identified on British maps as Fosse Wood, Walter's half-dug trench was the furthest any Englishman could go, the very edge of the English-speaking universe. As far as my search for Walter was concerned, this was the full distance, the end.

A bird, frightened by some twitch or leaf-fall, clattered up through the branches behind me and I turned in time to see a pigeon escape into the cloudless summer sky.

Milne says categorically that the battle to breach the Hindenburg Line – the battle that became known as the Battle of Bellenglise – was won by the guns:

> The concentration of artillery was probably the biggest in the history of the world. The guns stood wheel to wheel, rank on rank, as far as the eye could see. Walking back to Brigade when they were registering was much more terrifying than the battle . . . the result was that at Zero hour the heavens rained shells and the impregnable Hindenburg Line made of

ferro-concrete trenches was entirely and completely smashed. The behaviour of the infantry was magnificent, but without the guns they could never have obtained their objectives and held them, even with the help of the fog. Besides smashing the German trenches, the bombardment smashed the German morale . . . Some of the German infantry had been unable to leave their deep dugouts for forty-eight hours owing to the bombardment, and the stench in the dugouts was enough to make any German surrender.

Artillery conquers, infantry occupies. The British gunners who smashed the Hindenburg Line were scarcely recognisable as the same bunch of learners who had perpetrated the calamity of the Somme. They had learned how to out-Bruchmuller Bruchmuller and landed a cannonade on the Hindenburg Line of unparalleled power and accuracy. Between 1200 hours, September 28th 1918, and 1200 hours September 29th 1918, the British artillery was officially reported to have fired 943,847 rounds of ammunition. In order to achieve this annihilating weight of destruction, and to exploit it, Staff work and co-ordination of all arms attained a peak of efficiency beyond anything evinced previously. The British Army, as long as it could be supplied, was unstoppable.

Winston Churchill in *The World Crisis* says he knew the game was up for the Kaiser, but for slightly different reasons.

On [September] 28th [he writes] Bulgaria agreed uncondi-
tionally to demobilize her army, to restore all conquered territory, to surrender all means of transport, to cease to be a belligerent, and to place her railways and her territories at the disposal of the Allies for their further operations. I was in Paris with Loucheur [the French Minister of Armaments] when the news arrived, and it was recognised at once that the

end had come. On September 29th a Conference convened at Spa on Ludendorf's initiative decided to approach President Wilson, whose 'high ideals' fostered hope, with proposals on behalf of Germany for an armistice.

As with the news of Bulgaria's entry into the Great War, so with its exit. Both went unrecorded in the annals of the Leicestershire Regiment. Behind the lingering smoke of the barrage, untouched by diplomacy, ignorant of politics, hungry, thirsty, blinkered by the burden of their sorely tried humanity, Walter and 'D' Company carried on digging. As night fell on Fosse Wood on Sunday, September 29th 1918, it was Walter Butterworth who held the field. The guns had smashed the Hindenburg Line but it was the British infantry, settling down for another night of watching and waiting, who would win the War in six weeks' time. They had refused not the one great gesture of their times. All they had to do was hang on just a little while longer, and it would soon be over.

Cycling downhill from Magny la Fosse, heading for the café at the Riqueval Bridge where my family was waiting, my attention was caught by something at the side of the road. A crew of road-menders had recently passed by, leaving a smooth black surface to ride on but also gouging clean new edges to the cornfields. I thought at first glance that it was an old paint tin, or a rusty bucket which had been punched with holes to make a brazier. In that rich earth, a ditcher's thrust revealed . . . an English infantryman's helmet.

I rubbed off the dried mud and turned the helmet dish-ways up. Some fibres of the old leather webbing still adhered inside. Three neat holes and a jagged tear showed where the shrapnel had gone through.

I joined my family at the Riqueval Bridge Café. I'd had nothing to eat or drink all day, just a couple of peaches and a squashed croissant. I sank a glass of cold beer immediately, and then two more in quick succession. Then I unwrapped the buckled helmet from the plastic bag that I'd found to protect it.

'You mean this was a real helmet?' said Phoebe. 'On a real soldier?'

'An English soldier.'

Phoebe put a sugar-pink finger into a jagged rent and wiggled it.

'Did he die?'

'These holes are where the shrapnel went in.'

'Mummy said we could have an ice cream.'

I had found everything I'd been looking for, and more. Ice creams all round. We strapped my bike on to the back of the car, placed the unknown warrior's helmet in the rear window and headed for St Quentin. There was just one more thing.

'I thought you said you'd found him,' said my wife. 'You said you'd finished.'

She stopped the car and we stepped into a field of corn stubble with a gentle uphill slope.

'This is it—'

The obelisk was mounted on a plinth protected by a low chain. Brambles sprawled over the ground, giving the impression that the site wasn't looked after very well:

In memory of the officers, NCO's and men of the 46th (North Midland) Division (T.F.) who gave their lives for their country at Ypres ★ Hohenzollern Redoubt ★ Gommecourt ★ Lens ★ Bellenglise ★ Ramicourt ★ Mannequin Hill and Audigny-les-Fermes. Also, to commemorate the victory of 29th September, 1918, when the Division attacked the canal between Riqueval bridge and Bellenglise and broke through the Hindenburg Line, taking over 4,000 prisoners and 70 guns.

From the North Midland Division's memorial I could see across the valley that hid the St Quentin Canal to Ascension Ridge, where the Leicesters were plodding towards Riqueval. The battlefield lay stretched out like a counterpane. I could see where the Americans and Australians were still enmeshed in the coils of the Hindenburg Outpost Line. Coming up the slope towards me was the crashing wave of fire and steel that was the British barrage.

Phoebe found a ladybird on a blackberry leaf, Gabriel found a matchbox to keep it in. I took a photograph of Walter's great-grandchildren and turned for home.

12

HEART OF ENGLAND

They shall not return to us, the resolute, the young,
The eager and whole-hearted whom we gave . . .
                    Rudyard Kipling, 'Mesopotamia'

Blighty was the usual anti-climax. Stale air gushed into our faces as we opened the front door. The doormat was covered with brown envelopes, the cups in the sink had sprouted fungus. At the traffic lights, on my way to the 'all-nite' grocery for milk and bread, a police car thrashed past like a blue banshee, reminding me that in France I hadn't heard a siren in nearly three weeks. At Stockwell tube station beggars and junkies gave me the evil eye. Home is where the hurt is, London SW9; avoid contact, keep moving.

Back at the day job – 'Hi, Chris! Been anywhere interesting?' – I found that a new crew of bosses had seized control. We had been appropriated in a corporate takeover and rationalisation was in the air. Some said five jobs were to go, others said nine. The troops told each other to keep their heads well below the parapet.

The language of the trenches was on everyone's lips, lions led by donkeys. The news itself, our stock in trade, remained unchanged: the tribes were still killing each other; the presidents were making speeches; planes kept falling out of the sky.

My lunch-hour stroll took me by Australia House, the sculptured portal of which has long been a favourite Great War touchstone, opened by the King-Emperor, George V, wearing Field Marshal's uniform, in 1919. To the right of the entrance two old giants study scrolls before a magnificently breasted nubile arising from sleep, the personification of the Dream Time, *Terra Incognita Australis.* On the other side stand two young Titans and their open-eyed sister distributing the spoils which accrue once Australia's fertility has been realised by the sons of Empire. Signed 'Harold Parker, Sc. 1915–18.' I have always admired Harold's strength and boldness, the precision with which he's hewn each allegorical block to fit the exact anatomy of its neighbours. For three years, while the British Empire wrestled in the mud, Harold Parker carried on chiselling. I imagined him in his stone-yard in winter, muffled against the frost and snow – or perched on his summer scaffold, scrawny and vestless, hammering late into the night in a lather of sweat. Harold Parker reminded me that, even at the height of the struggle, many men were able to avoid the realities of the Great War.

It's a debate I'd like to hear one of these days: who did more for European civilization, 1914–1918 – those who fought or those who stayed away? Step forward, Walter Butterworth; advance, you faceless millions. It was a willingness to see things simply, to do or die, that saved the sum of things worth saving.

The township of Sains du Nord, where the Great War ended for the Fifth Leicesters, was six miles short of the Belgian border. The Fifth Leicesters reached it on November 9th 1918.

Those inhabitants who hadn't been killed or kidnapped by the retreating Germans turned out with whatever blooms came to hand. Says Hills:

> They thronged the streets with flags and great bunches of chrysanthemums, so that by the time we reached the Mairie we looked like a walking flower show ... We billeted in a large factory which had been used as a Hospital, while Battalion and Company Headquarters occupied various magnificent Châteaux.

The Fifth Leicesters stayed in Sains on November 10th, unable to move because their transport had been held up to the rear. The Germans had mined all the roads, uprooted the railways and demolished the bridges. Every movable thing of value had been looted. For Hills, the eager agent of British retribution, news of the Armistice came as a disappointment:

> All day long reports came in from the east showing the hopeless state of confusion to which the German Army had come. Civilians told us of artillery drawn by cows, airmen reported roads congested with traffic and columns of troops. It really looked as though at last we should have a chance of delivering a crushing blow. Late that night came the telegram ending hostilities, and the chance was gone for ever.

On the eleventh hour of the eleventh day of the eleventh month of 1918, the Great War between Germany and the rest of the world passed into abeyance. Some celebrated by getting drunk or shooting in the air, many slumped into apathy or depression. They had survived, but for what? It was difficult to imagine what Peace might mean now that War had become the accepted order.

The Leicesters were set to work filling in shell-holes and cleaning up the battlefields. Their officers tried to distract them with sports and theatrical amusements, but the weather was bad and now that the Germans had been beaten everyone was impatient to get home. Only one battalion per division would be needed for the occupation of the Rhineland. Hills was disappointed that the Fifth Leicesters weren't chosen. He had taken a liking to soldiering and, as demobilisation proceeded, he made sure that he was appointed to command the cadre – 5 officers and 46 men who stayed together to escort the Fifth Battalion's Colours back to England.

By June 30th 1919, Walter was back in Hinckley and the Colours of the Fifth Leicesters were hanging in Loughborough Town Hall. The first men to be demobilised had been those with jobs waiting for them in what were regarded as essential industries – coal, transport, agriculture. Each man was given his back pay and a rail warrant, and some got a gratuity, according to rank and length of service. Officers got more than men, generals got the most. The Commander-in-Chief, Sir Douglas Haig, was given an earldom, an equestrian statue in Whitehall and a lump sum of £100,000 – which he accepted reluctantly, having asked originally for twice as much. Among the public at large, the War's most obvious legacy was mass mutilation. Apart from the 1 million men who were dead and gone, a further 2½ million had been wounded. Over 40,000 male arms and legs had been removed from circulation, and more than 60,000 eyeballs. Twenty years later, as Britain girded herself for the Second World War, some 600,000 men were still claiming disability pensions from the First.

The idea of the 'Lost Generation' took root quickly. Writers like J.B. Priestley attested that their dead comrades had been the tragic flower of the country's manhood:

All the Armies in that idiot war shovelled divisions into attacks
... but the British command specialized in throwing men
away for nothing. The tradition of an officer class, defying
both imagination and common sense, killed most of my
friends as surely as if those cavalry generals had come out of
the châteaux with polo mallets and beaten their brains out.

Such loss, calculated as talent squandered, could not but lead to a
serious enfeeblement of the race. It seemed self-evident: 10 per
cent of Englishmen under 45 years of age had been eradicated.
In fact, the English had got off lightly. In a final tally of Great
War casualties, the British Empire was ranked eighth out of
ten. France, Russia, Germany and Italy had all lost more men,
proportionately, than Britain. Top of the league for casualties was
the Austro-Hungarian Empire: 90 per cent of its mobilised forces
had been killed, wounded or captured – a total of 7 million men.
Think of 100 Wembley Stadiums crammed to capacity. Then
remember that the total killed among all combatants, something
like 10 million, was less than the number who died in India alone
(16 million) during the great influenza pandemic of 1917–1918.

The 'Lost Generation' myth flourished because the cost of
the Great War to the British was not to be counted in gross
military casualties, nor in the amount of materiel consumed, nor
the quantity of gold expended. The cost of the Great War was a
deep and persistent sense of bereavement in the breast of every
citizen. At the outbreak of Peace, 2 million parents woke up to
the realisation that their sons were gone for ever, not just for the
duration. Every town and village, every street, was in mourning.

For veterans like Walter, the Great War marked a permanent loss
of faith in once-respected institutions. The name for this sour taste
was Disillusion, its chief literary exponent was C.E. Montague.
His slim volume, *Disenchantment*, caught the authentic mood of

Victory in the men who'd won it. It was a mixture of pride, grief and indignation:

> A man was a fool if he imagined that anyone set over him was not looking after number one; the patriotism of the press was bunkum, screening all sorts of queer games; the eloquence of patriotic orators was just a smoke barrage to cover their little manoeuvres against one another; the red tabs of the Staff were the 'Red Badge of Funk'; a hospital ward full of sick men would exchange, when left to themselves, vitriolic surmises about the extravagant pay that the nurses were probably getting, and go on to suggest what vast profits the YMCA must be making out of its huts. Wherever the contrary had not been proved to their own senses, the slacking, self-seeking and shirking that had muddled and spoilt their own training for war until they were put, half-trained, into the hottest of the fire must be assumed to be in authority everywhere . . . the lions felt they had found out the asses.

Those who had seen only the later stages of the War were still capable of remembering it as a good thing, and many survivors looked back on their War memories happily for the rest of their lives. Battle could be a transcendant experience, those who came through it knew they were unlikely ever again to feel the overwhelming self-realisation unleashed by combat. Nor was there any substitute for the sublime importance a man felt in battle, when his coolness might mean the difference between life and death for himself and his team. When the return to Civy Street was over, men mourned the ideal of companionship as much as the individual companions they'd lost.

Robert Graves says it took years to shake off his Army habits. After the War, he found it quite natural to lie, to steal, to scan the countryside with an eye to the positioning of machine guns, to break into unselfconscious conversation with strangers on trains, to pee by the roadside without shame. I wanted to know about Walter. Had he come back from the War with nightmares? Had he taken to gambling or binges? How had he changed? How had he rebuilt himself?

I went home to Leicester for the weekend of October 13th because according to Milne that was one of the two dates chosen by the city to commemorate its own very specific contributions to the Great War, namely the suicidal charge against the Hohenzollern Redoubt and the triumphant storming of the Hindenburg Line at Bellenglise:

> The laurel wreath of the 17th Regiment of Foot is still unbroken. The sun still shines on the Magazine and the poplar tree stands by its gate like some giant sentinel in Lincoln green. And on the 29th September and the 13th October each year the Union Jack flies jauntily from the mast-head. But nobody takes much notice of it; few realise why it is hoisted; but there are some who look at it wistfully, for they know what a struggle it was to keep it there.

Leicester's ancient Magazine served as the peacetime headquarters of the Fourth Leicesters. It had been built in the fourteenth century as a gatehouse to the ecclesiastical settlement which was at the heart of the medieval town. It was to this cobbled vault, under the gaze of its broken-nosed archers and halberdiers, that Captain Milne and the Fourth Leicesters had reported for duty in August 1914:

> In and out came Majors, Captains, Subalterns . . . Waiting

about stood boys who had just left Public Schools and were seeking vacant commissions . . . Up and down the stone steps ran Orderly Room Sargeant, and Clerk, Sargeant-Major, and Quartermaster . . . On an oblong table in the centre of the room lay mobilisation orders in red paper covers to which a white label proclaiming them secret was attached . . . Horses were requisitioned . . . and half-a-dozen bakers' carts for carrying ammunition . . . Very little was done in the way of medical inspections, which was a pity, and bayonets were not sharpened, which did not matter.

Now, three generations later, I peered through a thick glass door into the same Orderly Room and found it deserted. The Magazine had been converted into the Museum of the Leicestershire Regiment during the Sixties, I had come to see the Victoria Cross which Lieutenant John Barrett had won at Pontruet. A letter taped to the glass door explained that the Museum was shut because it was about to be extensively refurbished with a grant of Lottery money. The same letter had been there on two previous visits: 'Staff intend to brighten the appeal of the current displays to include the social and military history of both conflict and peace time, and the lives of the soldiers of the Regiment and their families . . .'

Where the Orderly Sergeant's table had stood was a workman's trestle. In place of the secret orders for mobilisation lay a surveyor's folded blueprint. White patches on the walls showed where pictures and display cases had been removed; dust lay thickly. There was no poplar standing sentinel in Lincoln green, no jaunty Union Jack a-flutter, not even a flagpole. Leicester's Magazine, once fought over by Cavaliers and Roundheads, had been turned into a traffic island, approachable only through a maze of pedestrian subways. I doubted that when the Magazine's refurbishment had been completed, if ever, there would be much space devoted to events at the Hohenzollern Redoubt and Bellenglise. There were no Leicesters left to argue the case. That fine fighting breed, the Leicestershire Terrier, was extinct. The Seventeenth Regiment of Foot, the Leicestershire Regiment, had gone west in 1964, amalagamated into oblivion like the rest. Of the 69 Regiments of the Line that were fighting in France and Flanders in 1915, barely a handful remain.

A big black cannon captured by the Leicesters in the Crimean War pointed down Oxford Street, now a five-lane artery in modern Leicester's traffic system. Milne would have recognised the grimy factory on the right no doubt, but not the building opposite, the city's erstwhile Congregational Chapel. It was still there, but under heavy disguise. A congregation of Jains had Disneyfied the austere brick building into a cartoonist's idea of an oriental temple.

I left the Magazine, following the first footsteps that the Fourth Leicesters had taken towards the Western Front. August 12th 1914, had been one of the hottest days of the year, and some of the older men wilted under the unaccustomed weight of Field Service Marching Order, plus extra ammunition. The Duke and Duchess of Rutland had turned up to say goodbye, among others: 'There is a group of elderly gentlemen on the steps of the Leicestershire Club,' says Milne, 'they are the employers of some of the men in the ranks; they look and they wonder; they wonder what will be the end of it all.'

I marched down Newarke Street, past vacant lots and the shells of old factories appropriated by Leicester Polytechnic. The two buildings that remained wholly intact from the Great War era, the Magazine Hotel and the Leicestershire Club, only confirmed what had been lost. The hotel was closed for refurbishment as a seven-day-a-week 'Pub Rock' venue; the Leicestershire Club was trading under new management as a de-luxe 'Pub Grub' outlet.

231

TRENCH FEVER

I stood on the same stone steps whence the Fourth Leicesters' civilian employers had watched their clerks and shift-hands march off to war. I looked down the straight length of Newarke Street towards the Magazine for a glimpse of the khaki ranks of August 1914. They tramped by invisibly, marching badly, sweating in their itchy uniforms, red-faced and self-conscious under the whoops of the non-existent shop-girls and millwrights hanging out of their long-demolished windows:

> People swarm around the troops [says Milne], shouting farewell to their sons, sweethearts and friends; shouting to anyone and everyone, for in this time of crisis everyone speaks to his neighbour. An old, dirty-looking woman accosts a young officer as he marches in front of his Company. 'I shall be waiting for you when you come back, me duck,' she cries. He has never seen her before and he hopes he never will again, but the words stick in his memory . . . The Fourth Leicestershires leave their native town praying that they may get to France before the war is over. And the elderly gentlemen at the Leicestershire Club walk slowly down its steps to their business, still wondering what will be the end of it all.

'The only time I remember your grandad talking about the War,' said Uncle Mick, 'were when Ernie Bedford came round to lay a concrete path in the back garden of Factory Road. He says to me, "He's a good 'un, our Ernie. We was blown up together in the trenches. I were buried up to me chest, but Ernie went under right up to his chin."'

My mother and I were sitting in Uncle Mick's neat front room in Sunnyside, Hinckley. It was the house where Uncle Mick and Auntie Phyllis had lived ever since I could remember. It was

232

where, as an eight-year-old, I used to play on the carpet during Christmas visits.

'I'll tell you summat about your grandad,' said Uncle Mick. 'He would never hear a rude word said against anyone. If me and your Uncle Pete started singing our Army songs after we'd had a few pints he used to shush us up quick. "Pack it in, right now," he'd say. "If yer Mam catches hold of that, we'll all be for it."'

I said I had heard that, with Walter, it was 'bugger this' and 'bugger that' all day long.

'I'm talking about rude words,' said Uncle Mick. 'Bugger ain't a rude word. You show me someone as don't say bugger, bloody or damn . . .'

Uncle Mick was the image of his mother, Clara. I remembered her quite clearly – tall and thin, with a Park Drive cigarette always on the go. Clara's skin, before she died, took on the parchment hue of nicotine. Every time you made Hinckley Grandma laugh, she told you to stop because it made her cough. What with Clara being so tall and Walter being so short, they must have made an odd couple.

'I'll tell you this, our Christopher, your grandad were the best mate I ever had. We had some great fun. You ask anybody in Hinckley and they'll all say, "Walter? He were one of the best." And I'll tell you summat else, I didn't half miss him when he died. I still do . . .'

Uncle Mick had worked most of his life in what turned out to be the last big shoe factory in Hinckley, J.V. Finn's. He had joined the firm shortly after coming back from Palestine, where he'd served during the Second World War. He stayed at Finn's until he retired at the age of 65. There was no speech, no collection, no pension when he left. Uncle Mick signed off after 40 years with hardly a goodbye – and Finn's shut down for good a few months after.

'Walter now,' said Uncle Mick, 'he died the week afore he were due to collect his pension. Clara found him. He'd brought her a cup of tea in bed, same as always, and gone back down to the kitchen and collapsed. When she found him, she went running down to the police station to get the lodger – they were letting out the front room of Factory Road to lodgers then, he were a policeman – and the lodger came up and he said, "Yes, he's dead, it's a heart attack." And that were that. So listen to this: the next week George Bennett comes round to the house, Walter's boss. And he says to Clara how sad he were, and what a good foreman Walter had been, and how much he'd done for the firm, and so on. And could he give her summat? Well, it were an envelope. And in the envelope was thirty-seven quid.' Uncle Mick let this sink in. 'That's a pound for each year that Walter had worked at Bennett's in Barwell.'

Maybe he wasn't so different from Walter. Since he'd retired Mick had filled out more. He looked proud and indignant.

'It were sod all, weren't it?' said Uncle Mick. 'Even for them days. A pound a year! Chap gives you his working life and you go round to slip his widder thirty-seven quid? Bloody cheek! That's what they think of us, the buggers.'

Uncle Mick, renowned throughout his family for being a good laugh, found it necessary to look out of the window for a couple of seconds to collect himself. In that moment, I saw how we really were: two grown men caught up in something beyond our control.

'You see,' said Uncle Mick, 'once you get to my age you look back and you see things you didn't see before. You think, "Bloody hell, it's gone. Life's passed me by and I didn't even notice."'

Death. Death was everywhere. From Uncle Mick's house I went to the plot in Hinckley Cemetery where the ashes of Walter Noël Gordon Butterworth were buried:

'Died March 25th 1940, aged 25 years, at rest.'

It had never occurred to me, until I stood in front of his grave, that Walter Noël Gordon had been my uncle as much as any of the others.

'Our Gordon were born on the twenty-fifth,' said Uncle Mick, 'and he died on the twenty-fifth. He were twenty-five when he died, and I'm not sure that he weren't sick with the T.B. for twenty-five weeks before that. It knocked my Mam and Dad for six when our Gord went.'

I checked the newspaper archive:

COLLAPSED AND DIED AT HIS HOME

Mr Walter Brown Butterworth (63), 25 Factory Road, Hinckley, collapsed and died at his home early today. Mr Butterworth, well-known in boot and shoe circles, had recently been elected unopposed Vice-President of the Hinckley Working Men's Club. (*Leicester Mercury*, March 19th 1956.)

BUTTERWORTH, Walter Brown. Factory Road, Hinckley, aged 64, passed away suddenly at home, Monday March 19th, 1956. Cremation, Leicester Gilroes, Thursday March 22nd, 12 noon. (No flowers by request.) Further inquiries to Messrs. Geo. Sellers, Funeral Director. Phone Hinckley 457. (*Leicester Mercury*, March 20th 1956.)

I went to Auntie Jean's house where my mother was waiting for me, drinking tea. I found myself sneaking looks at both sisters for the purpose of comparison: each was a version of Clara Butterworth — both widowed, both tea addicts, both grandmas. Auntie Jean announced, between puffs at her Park Drive cigarette, that she had just paid the final instalment of her funeral plan —

the one she'd taken out with Messrs George Sellers, Hinckley's foremost funeral directors. Her instructions to her children, she said, were that her ashes were to be scattered in Burbage Wood at bluebell time.

In the days of the Roman occupation of Britain, the geographical heart of England – *Anglicae Cor* – was reckoned to be the intersection of the province's two great highways, the Watling Street (London to Chester) and the Fosse Way (Bath to Lincoln). This intersection was a couple of miles from Burbage Wood on the southern edge of Hinckley, the town motto of which is '*Anglicae Cor*'. Siegfried Sassoon passed by in 1913, during the height of his fox-hunting mania, and records the impression made by Hinckley on his upper-class hero, Norman Loder: '. . . after skirting a straggling and ill-favoured town which was, I had gathered, mainly addicted to the manufacture of boots, he suddenly exclaimed – "They never ought to have built a place like that so near Burbage Wood!"'

'When we were young,' said my mother, coasting downhill into Smockington Hollow in her bumbling little car, 'your grandad used to bring us out here on a Sunday, picking bluebells, or blackberries . . . We'd be gone all day . . . Couldn't do it now, look at the traffic . . .'

'What about you?' I asked. 'Do you want your ashes to be scattered in Burbage Wood?'

'No,' she said. 'I want to be buried. You can cremate me if you want, but keep my ashes together. I want to know that I'll be somewhere definite after I've gone.'

In a little gravel car park we found the remains of the High Cross of England, the latest in a long succession of monuments marking the intersection of Watling Street and Fosse Way. Two and a half centuries of lightning and thunder had reduced it to a patched heap of rubble. Of the graffiti-scarred inscription only the ironic words *'perpetuam Memoriam'* could still be deciphered. I hopped over a gate and walked a few steps down the Fosse Way toward Leicester.

The word 'Fosse' ran through my brain like a mantra, referring me to the trenches of that name which Walter and the Fifth Leicesters had dug all over the Western Front. From the sensory evidence, I might easily have been in Artois or Picardy. The grass was the same, the trees, the bird-song . . . I tried to spot the best places for my machine guns and my forward observation posts. This landscape refused to accommodate my imagined Great War; it was home.

On my mother's side, the inheritance of 'Home' came to me from Walter Butterworth. He had paid the price of his generation. On my dead father's side, these fields came to me collaterally through my Uncle Reg, farmer of this parish. They were his cows that grazed the Fosse Way. That was his house I could see from the High Cross of England. Uncles, cousins; mothers, sons. I had never lived in Hinckley, but I would always be a part of it.

Doubt crept in at the end, as it tends to do: had I really 'found' Walter? Perhaps the quiet satisfaction I had felt at Riqueval Bridge was just that – a feeling, not a fact. I knew there was no way of knowing for sure where Walter was on September 29th 1918, when the Fifth Leicesters broke the Hindenburg Line. The Great War's greatness did not allow for certainties in the matter of individual combatants in major battles. But I knew also that if I hadn't found Walter at Riqueval, I must have met him somewhere else – among the blackened stumps of Sanctuary Wood, or the grassy declivities of the Talus des Zouaves? Or Fosse Wood . . . ?

Leicester Fosse had been Walter's team. Fosse 8 had been his Calvary. Fosse Wood had been his triumph. And here was Fosse Way, bringing me back to where it all began, to the Anglo-Saxon virtues which had prevailed on the Western Front. Honour. Justice. Wherever I might go in the wide world, I was rooted in the heart of England.